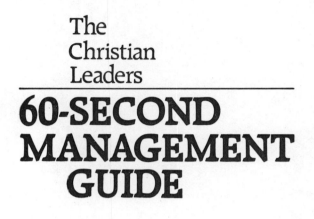

The
Christian
Leaders

60-SECOND
MANAGEMENT
GUIDE

Other Word Books by the Same Authors . . .

The Art of Management for Christian Leaders

The Christian Executive

The
Christian
Leaders

60-SECOND MANAGEMENT GUIDE

Ted W. Engstrom
Edward R. Dayton

WORD BOOKS
PUBLISHER
WACO, TEXAS

A DIVISION OF
WORD, INCORPORATED

Library of Congress Cataloging in Publication Data

Dayton, Edward R.
   The Christian leader's 60-second management guide.

   1. Christian leadership.   I. Engstrom, Theodore
Wilhelm, 1916–   II. Title.   III. Title: Christian
leader's sixty-second management guide.
BV652.1.D39   1984   254   84-5159
ISBN 0-8499-0396-3

Printed in the United States of America

Contents

The Other Side of Management

There are all kinds of books about what managers *should* do. This is a book about what managers really do.

There are many books about what Christian leaders *ought* to do and be. This is a book about the everyday problems that every Christian leader faces.

It's a book about principles, things like competence and integrity and authority.

It's a book about getting along with people, motivating them, encouraging them, leading them.

It's a book about the tensions in the everyday life of a leader—interruptions, Murphy's Law, finding a new secretary.

Life is full of decisions. It only takes a minute—sixty seconds—to make wrong ones and right ones. Sixty seconds. Sixty seconds in which an entire future may be decided. Sixty seconds to gather up all the wisdom and experience gained in a lifetime and put them to work.

Life is made up of all of these minute-by-minute sixty-second decisions. It's our hope that this book will guide you as a Christian leader in a life that will be more pleasing to you and more pleasing to God.

EDWARD R. DAYTON
TED W. ENGSTROM

The
Christian
Leaders

60-SECOND
MANAGEMENT
GUIDE

:01

Manager or Minister?

Minister or manager? Unfortunately, too many Christian organizations are led by men or women who have a gift for ministry and little training (or perhaps even an inclination) for management. Witness the large number of leaders of Christian organizations who are ordained. Of course, ordination does not exclude a person having management gifts and skills, but it does give an indication of the leader's basic training and probable bias. The emphasis is on ministry.

But assuming that we have selected the best managers that we can find to lead the organization, do we not still have a responsibility to minister to each other? Of course.

A Manager As Minister

Even a hardened army top sergeant knows that people are the ultimate key to a successful organization. A great deal of thought and study has been given to make people more productive. Giving them more satisfying work, providing adequate remuneration, placing them in an environment which is conducive to their well-being, and helping them to feel good about themselves, the organization and their task, are among the most successful means. Most of the management literature indicates that all of this is done for the good of the organization, or for the good of the product. This is probably only a half-truth. Most men and women, be they Christian or non-Christian, enjoy helping others and seeing others operate effectively. And as a society, we seem to be learning about the innate responsibility of organizations to society.

11

But what about the Christian manager? If he or she is leading an organization made up of members of the same mystical Body of which he or she is a part, is there not some special relationship implied?

What guidelines can we give?

If the organization is to survive, ultimately the organization must have first priority. There will be times when the organization will permit itself to be diverted from its task for the good of the individual. However, if the leadership of the organization believes that the organization exists as a part of God's purpose, eventually the tragic choice between the good of the organization and the good of one individual must be settled in favor of the organization. (We are assuming that every Christian organization has a fundamental responsibility for people.)

It does not follow that the manager never puts aside purposes for people. Most situations which will face the Christian manager will not be a clear-cut question of the choice between the organization and the individual. Usually they will be situations in which he or she can respond to the need of an individual without jeopardizing the organization. But nevertheless, the purpose is what the organization exists for.

How do we minimize the tension between caring for people and accomplishing our goals?

Start with the selection of staff. There are three common reasons why individuals seek to join a Christian organization: First, they may have a strong belief in the organization's purposes. Second, they may be attracted by the idea of working with other Christians in an environment which is usually less competitive and where, by definition, people are more likely to be concerned for the individual as a person. Third, there will be those who come to work in the Christian organization because for one reason or another they could not succeed in a secular organization. Too often, the Christian organization's lower salary structure is such that it tends to attract people in this last category.

Go for excellence! Look for the best people whom you can find. Concentrate on those who have a high sense of Christian calling balanced by the necessary skills and experience. One is not a replacement for the other. Both are needed.

Demonstrate in your own lifestyle what you expect of others. Model the desired characteristics of how the business of the organization ought to be carried out. The marks of a Christian organization are intangible. Simply because a gospel text is on the wall doesn't make the organization effectively Christian. Rather it is a spirit that is evident among the people, a spirit that is constantly engendered, prayed for, and again modeled by those who are to set the pace.

Encourage members of the organization to minister to each other. Help them learn to respond to felt needs, moving into situations carefully and cautiously, guided by the Holy Spirit.

Recognize that you are an authority figure. We need to remember that although we are Christian brothers and sisters, the manager or leader is a very significant person in the life of the staff members. We are responsible for the person's well-being to the extent of his salary and working situation. There is an authoritative role that is forced upon each manager. Some of your staff will feel more "ministered to" if they see you as acting in the role of a peer. Others will need a father (or mother!) figure. The latter have a need to know that someone is in charge and that their personal welfare is in good hands.

Don't use "Christian" manipulation. Because many staff members are highly motivated to be workers in God's kingdom, we may be tempted to use this motivation inappropriately. Because they are doing the "Lord's work" does not give us license to take advantage of the individual's personal time. We must be careful not to expect our staff to work consistent unpaid overtime, nor accept all our pronouncements as divinely inspired.

Finally, be a lover. "Love God and do as you please." This suggestion made by St. Augustine assumes that if we loved the Lord with all our mind and heart and strength, what pleases us would please Him. How do we know we love God? By how we treat each other. "A new commandment I give you: Love one another. . . . All men will know that you are my disciples if you love one another" (John 13:34–35, NIV). Jesus said that. We can't improve on it.

13

:02

What Good Managers Know

Good managers are not confined to any one field or single occupation. It is a truism of management that a good manager is a good manager wherever he or she may be operating.

Good managers know that the health of an organization is **Commitment** based upon a series of commitments among the members of the organization and between the members of the organization and those outside of it. Commitments often become viable only when they are in writing. At the heart of the old adage "If it isn't in writing, it doesn't exist" is the understanding that commitments must be recorded—they must be observable by a third party. It is not a question of not trusting another's word. Rather, it is a recognition that the life of an organization is an ongoing process. For new staff to understand where their predecessors were going, they must be able to review the commitments made by them. In our computerized world this is recognized as documentation. If someone is going to modify a program, they must understand the program. What is so easily understood about inanimate machines is even more true for people.

A commitment is an agreement on the part of one person to reach a mutually agreed upon objective. An objective, or a goal, is a statement of a future condition or event that includes the time when it will become a past event. In other words, a goal can be achieved. None of us make commitments about the past. All commitments lie in the future. (See Chapter 10.) So good managers know that they manage best by seeking written commitments from others. 15

Good managers know that they have numerous commitments: commitments to themselves, to their subordinates, to their peers, and to their superiors. Obviously, the Christian manager sees all four of these commitments under the lordship of Christ. One's ability to recognize these four types of commitments and to manage them is what differentiates the experienced manager from the inexperienced manager. For these commitments to be managed, they must be first agreed to by the four sets of people involved. Since situations will continually change, these commitments will also need to be reaffirmed with the passage of time.

Types of Commitment

Commitments to ourselves and our calling will change in the process of time. As one goal is reached, others will replace it. These commitments, goals and statements of faith about our future are the source of our vision and dreams. Therefore it is helpful to put them in writing so we can evaluate our progress.

Commitments to our subordinates will also change as various goals are reached. There will be new plans to be made, and new endeavors to be undertaken. It is to be hoped that we have learned from both our successes and failures and are ready to build on them.

Commitments between peers begin to change as the organization changes with time. A new set of commitments will be required between those who work alongside one another. Organizations are seldom static. They change just as the people in them do.

And in the same way that we expect commitments from our subordinates, so we have *commitments to our superiors.* These, too, will change.

Failure of Commitment

Good managers know that it's seldom possible for a manager or the people working for him or her to fully understand all of the implications of their failing to meet their commitments. It is very easy for the individual to become so concerned with his own situation that he abandons or modifies his original commitments for others he feels are more important. But the ramifications of their failure can ripple through an entire organization. "For want of a nail a shoe was lost, for want of a shoe the horse was lost. . . ."

Planning

Good managers know that for goals to be realistic they must be backed up by a program or plan for how the goal will be reached. Good managers know that the possibility of things going wrong far exceeds the possibility of things going right.

They know that any goal is the result of reaching a series of sub-goals. We call these steps plans or programs.

Good managers know that effective delegation is based upon a written plan. A plan is a request on the part of a subordinate for authority to proceed. It is the evidence that the subordinate knows how to achieve the hoped-for goal and that there is a way for measuring progress. In order to accept delegation four things are needed: 1) knowledge or skill, 2) understanding of what is requested, 3) a belief that it is in one's best interest, and 4) a belief that it is in the best interest of the organization. A plan written by the one who is to accept the task usually demonstrates that all four requirements have been met.

Good managers know that to manage commitments they must build a system of control (including self-control) that will produce timely information as to when there has been an apparent or real change in the commitment. This system must include self-control. When any party to the commitment has been unable to keep it, there must be enough time to enter into a new series of commitments that will benefit everyone involved.

Controls need to be designed as an integral part of a plan. In other words, when a subordinate submits a plan for approval, he or she should, at the same time, submit a plan for measuring progress. Control begins with measurement. Measurement begins with incorporating a system into the plan for achievement, which includes a plan for control.

Since virtually every task can be broken down into a series of events, one of the obvious places to start measuring is at the expected point of completion for each event. If there are ten events that have to happen in order for a goal to be reached, then one way of gaining control is to measure the progress of accomplishment at each of the ten events. Did it happen? If it didn't happen, when is it likely to happen?

Most managers recognize the need to plan for "big" events. Inexperienced managers fail to plan for the "small" events. They fail to realize that almost everything they do is interwoven with everything else. In the long run, planning and small events will more than compensate for the time it takes to do the planning.

Good managers know that management has to do with people. Inexperienced managers tend to think of management in terms of tasks. Good managers realize that an organization is like a body. Its health is dependent upon the health of each individual member. The right person in the right role, given the right tools and the right encouragement and training, is a key to good management.

Good managers recognize that developing an organization requires the development of people. They carry this out through a planned program of selecting the best people they can find, helping them to thoroughly learn their job, coaching them along the way and giving regular personal evaluation.

What Do Christian Managers Know?

A Christian organization is one that sees its ultimate purpose as giving glory to God through serving Christ. Good managers in Christian organizations know two more things.

First, they know there is a creative tension between depending on God and depending on oneself, between following well-laid plans and following the leading of the Holy Spirit. This tension is never resolved, nor should it be. We are dealing with something much greater than ourselves. To quote the words of Bishop Stephen Neill, "The game of life is played between the poles."

Second, good managers in Christian organizations have a quiet confidence that, regardless of what happens, however great the success or dismal the failure, God is at work to do His will. He is the One who is for us.

:03

What Good Managers Do

Management theory has to do with organizing, staffing, directing, controlling, communicating and a number of other functions required by modern organizations of almost any size.

If you have ever had the experience of keeping an hour-by-hour record of everything you did for a week, you have probably discovered that you would be hesitant to submit it as a case study on good management. What managers do every day can best be described as leading others, handling disturbances, acting as a figurehead, disseminating information, acting as a spokesman, negotiating with people, monitoring how things are going, and allocating resources. Many of us feel that practically everything we do is in response to some problem. We see ourselves as continually fighting fires.

What Managers Really Do

The interesting thing is that most managers like it that way. They enjoy the challenge of a new problem every hour or so, the ebb and flow of interruptions, the excitement of changed plans, new ideas. Oh, they would be happy if they had more time. They picture themselves as stretched between conflicting values. They feel guilty about not spending more time with their family and working in their church. They wish they could relax more. But when they do discover some better method of time management, more often than not they spend the time doing more of the same.

Managers Like It That Way

Most managers picture themselves as never having enough information. Consequently, almost every decision they face depends upon their ability to internally process whatever data

19

they have with their own experience. Often managers describe the rationale for their final decisions as a "hunch" or "feeling."

Management vs. the Manager

On the other hand, management is logical and rational. It seeks to anticipate the need it wants to fulfill, and factually describe that need along with the approaches necessary to meet it. There is a rather tacit assumption that if all the data were available, the solution would be obvious. It is essentially a problem-solving approach. It tends to avoid emotion and feeling, even though it recognizes that since business is carried out through people, "people problems" will have to be dealt with.

The popular management theory of MBO (Management by Objective) is a good reflection of this rational thinking. Overall purposes are formulated by the leadership of the organization. Major objectives (goals) are then assigned to functional units. All of these goals are future events, or desirable futures, that the leadership believes would be desirable in terms of outcome, be it money, product, service or even fellowship. The unit leader then sits down with key individuals and works out their personal objectives, which are supposedly supportive of the organization's objectives. Performance against these objectives (desirable future events) is then the measurement used to manage the operation. Deviation from the anticipated goal is viewed as a need to either modify the plan ("corrective action") or modify the goal.

But the future seldom conforms to our desires, particularly in detail. There seems to be a much greater chance that something will go wrong than right. Consider the baseball batter as an example. His usual "plan" is to get on base, normally by hitting the ball with the bat. But we call those who "fail" six times out of ten (those batting .400), heroes.

It is this unpredictability that challenges the manager. Most managers are attracted to management for this very reason.

The Big Picture vs. the Snapshot

Management theory is extremely useful in carrying out any enterprise. Those of us involved in the leadership of Christian organizations ignore it to the peril of the enterprise for which we may be responsible. We need clearly stated purposes, well-conceived goals, detailed plans, methods of evaluation and feedback. These are part of the big picture, the framework within which we have to operate.

But we also need people—people who, though they may be concerned with the big picture, are very much involved in the battle at hand. These people know that they are part of an important and meaningful enterprise. But they also realize that to achieve the ultimate purpose, they are going to be faced with a myriad of everyday changes, decisions, frustrations and hardships which are the mortar that makes the grand edifice possible.

The manager of the smaller agency or church or the middle manager of the larger enterprise has three kinds of time: *superior time, peer and subordinate time* and *discretionary time*. As far as his or her organizational life is concerned the manager has little or no control over time spent with superiors. The amount of time spent with peers and subordinates may be easier to control depending upon the structural style of the organization. Whatever time is left in the course of a day or week can be used at the manager's discretion. It is only in our discretionary time, the time directly under our control, that we as leaders can devote ourselves to the kind of reflection necessary to give us the big picture we need to intuitively process the data we have when we are faced with those daily fires. It is during this time that we can set our own personal goals and design plans to reach them.

Three Kinds of Time

Management theory recognizes this dilemma when it pictures the senior executive as spending a good deal of time in long-range planning, policy making, and in giving general guidance to the "ship." First-level managers are recognized as having very little time to carry out these functions. "Middle managers" fall somewhere in between. Whether you seem to be fighting too many fires or too few depends on where you are in the organizational structure. People at the head of an organization should have more discretionary time than others further down.

Levels of Discretionary Time

If you are a planning type of person, look for someone who is more of a firefighting kind of person to help you. If you are spending all your time in the midst of the fray, see what can be done to set aside time for prayer and contemplation of the future.

Where Are You?

Don't get hung up on the fact that every day does not go according to plan or that you are not the best time manager in the world. A predictable world would be pretty dull, anyway. On the other hand, dip into the literature that deals with the technique (as opposed to theory) of "time management." A great deal has been written about how to handle mail, interruptions, visitors, meetings, memos, conflicts, and a host of other experiences, more effectively.

21

:04

Least of All Saints

The Bible is replete with people who are put in positions of leadership and management. Their styles cover a wide range. Nehemiah the Planner, Peter the Impetuous, Jethro the Management Consultant, Lydia the House Church Leader. And Paul the Mover. Some of these men and women are more difficult to figure out than others. Some are well organized. Others seem to be anything but organized.

What a mixture Paul appears to be! The least of all saints who believed he was eminently qualified. On the one hand, able to bear all things. On the other hand, realizing that he had yet to achieve the goal that lay before him. Great sense of strength. Great sense of weakness. **Why Me?**

For many Christian leaders Paul's experience magnifies and models our own. Those of us who have been called to roles of leadership often say to ourselves, "Why did God do all of this for me? Why is He giving me these privileges of leadership?" There is a suspicion that not only are we really not deserving of God's grace, but we're really not that good at what we are doing anyway. Which man was the real Paul—the one who led so confidently or the one who was deeply uncertain of his abilities?

Most Christian leaders who have been tested in their role of leadership would probably answer, both! There is the agony and the ecstasy.

It is in the nature of humbleness that those who possess it are not supposed to know it.

True humbleness accepts this mixture of failure and success.

23

It sees that all is a result of God's grace. It balances Paul's "Surely you have heard about the administration of God's grace" that is linked with its subject, "given to me" and to its object, "for you" (Eph. 3:2).

True Humbleness

Much of our difficulty in finding a middle ground between self-confidence and complete dependence is the result of the beginning point in our thinking. For most Westerners, this beginning point is the individual—me. When we read Paul, we naturally relate to him as an individual because that's the way we think about the world. This can cause some real difficulties which another perspective may help.

Another Perspective

As Christians we get a better perspective on this apparent tension between what we are and what we are called to be if we first understand that leadership is a role and, second, that Christian leadership can only be defined within the context of the body of Christ.

Modern management theorists have attempted to isolate particular attributes of a leader. There have been many theories of leadership. But in the final analysis, all have failed to produce a coherent system. About the only definition that one can settle on is that "a leader is a person who has followers in a given situation." It is the context that establishes the leader, both the context of the situation and the context of those who are willing and able to follow his or her leadership.

The search for the common attributes of a Christian leader also fails. When we use the famous leaders of the Old and New Testament, we often overlook the fact that each of these men and women were called to a particular task for a particular group of people. Abraham was called to be the father of a nation. Moses was called to lead God's people, as were Joshua, the judges and the kings that followed. In the New Testament it is also the people of God, the body of Christ, who are the object of God's concern.

Overemphasis on the Individual

In our modern Western world, we tend to overemphasize the individual. We fail to see that we have been called out of our individualism into a community. All of our Western culture and training emphasizes the individual. It is the individual who is educated. It is the individual whose task is described by a job description. It is the individual who has to be motivated. Indeed, the immediate reaction of every Westerner to these sentences is something like, "Well, how else can you think about people if you don't think about individuals?" The fact that other societies, other cultures, may have an entirely different concept of "self" is quite beyond our comprehension.

24

It is part of our Christian understanding that none of us can *Least of All Saints* be any more than God cares to make of us. We talk about our being "clay in the potter's hand." But this seems to run contrary to the need to assert ourselves as leaders. We need a different understanding of leadership, one which doesn't lose the mystery of the sovereignty of God, or His grace, but which places us as Christian leaders in a more biblical perspective.

If leadership is only defined by followers and by the situation, **The** then the reason that leaders are "great" must be because they **Least** had great followers and the right situation. In other words, to **and** use biblical language, they were fitted together with others who **the** permitted them to play the role that God had assigned to them. **Greatest**

It is also apparent that none of us are leaders all of the time. Change the followers, change the context, and as far as anyone can tell, we are just another joint or ligament in this marvelous thing called the body of Christ.

In practice this is how most Christian organizations look for **The** new leaders—at least the individuals who will head the local **Way** church as pastor or the Christian organization as director or **It** president. We use such language as "called" to a pastorate. We **Works** tell one another that "God has provided the person we are seeking." Our job is to "discover" him or her.

But for others further back in the management/leadership stream, we may be less specific and more inclined not to emphasize spiritual gifts. Sometimes we even overlook the question of whether the followers of this new leader are fitted to him or her!

Thus we institutionalize the manager/leader role and divorce it both from the context of the organization and from the part of the body to which this person is to be joined.

As leaders we are the least of all saints. We are also people **What's** whom God has set apart for a special situation. Whether that **the** will still be our place and calling next week, next month or next **Point?** year, is not in our hands (or shouldn't be).

Consequently, the first question is not whether I am a good Christian leader, but whether I have been called and fitted into this organization for God's purpose at this time.

Second, if there is honor due, it is not to me, but to the role, the function, that I have been assigned to carry. (The same Bible that says honor your leaders also says that we, as the body of Christ, are to give honor to those parts least deserving of it.)

Last, there is the mystery and wonder of why God has chosen 25 to pour out His grace upon us. What a privilege it is to be the men and women whom He intends to use for His purposes in this day.

:05

So You Have a New Job

It is surprising how many men and women take a position in an organization without having a clear picture of their expected relationship to the organization and the people in it (or what is expected of them). This is particularly true in the case of the newly called pastor or other church staff member. Too often the desired "job description" for the pastor reads likes a combination of Dwight D. Eisenhower, the Apostle Paul, St. Francis of Assisi and Pope John Paul. Since few of us measure up to such a combination, the church obviously has to compromise something. The trouble is they may never identify what it is they are willing to give up. Therefore, the new pastor may become very frustrated trying to keep up with all of the expectations.

As a new staff person, your first task is to try to learn what is expected of you. This may not be as simple as it seems. What are you expected to accomplish? How will you and the organization know whether you have accomplished it or not? What are you *not* expected to do? What means and methods are considered appropriate within this organization for meeting goals? What are the norms of the organization; what is deemed appropriate and inappropriate? In other words, what is expected of everyone in the organization?

If the organization you have joined has not planned an orientation for you, usually no one will object if you help design one for yourself. There is general recognition that newcomers need to get acquainted with their new "home," and efforts on your part to try to understand the organization will usually be met with approval. Start with a question to your superior such as:

27

"Who are the key people I should be certain to talk with in order to understand this organization and my position in it?" After such a list has been prepared, ask a significant person within the organization to write a memo or a letter of introduction to each of the people with whom you are to meet. This letter should give some background as to your previous experience and what you have been called to do within the organization. This will save you a considerable amount of time making yourself known and will quickly establish to others where you "fit" into the total organizational structure.

**Write
a
Job
Description**

In this letter of introduction there will usually be a brief statement of what the position entails and what your responsibilities are. Many times it will include a complete job description. These are seldom static and seldom accurate. It is a good idea to meet with your superior or the group of people to whom you report and ask for their analysis of where they think this job description should be changed to reflect the current situation. You might want to review it yourself and see if there are some points which need clarification. What decisions are you expected to make? What decisions are you expected *not* to make? (This will give you some insight into the decision-making process within the organization.) Is the organization used to having unilateral authoritative decisions made by those in positions of leadership or are decisions usually reached by consensus?

What can the organization do, now that you are a part of it, that it could not do before? What immediate needs can be met because of who you are and what you know? Who is supposed to help you? Who is able to help you? (Later on you'll have to discover who will help you.)

**Learn
About
Your
Predecessor**

What kind of a person was your predecessor? What was his or her style? How did s/he go about making decisions? With whom did this person find the best relationships? You can learn such information by reviewing the correspondence carried over into your position, and by asking such questions as "What do you consider were Joe Jones' greatest assets and contributions to the organization?" (Do your best to avoid asking questions that will bring out negative discussions about your predecessor. You'll hear about those all too soon.)

Continually asking this question will garner all kinds of information for you. If the goals of the organization seem to be unclear, many times you can help to bring them into focus. Then you can concentrate on the ones which, by your own experience and capabilities, are particularly attractive to you. By discussing the organization's goals with the different members of the organization, you can help take attention away from the details of the job and focus them on the major purpose of the job.

Don't be afraid to take the lead and make decisions in the area of bringing people together to set goals and make plans. Just stay within the limits of your responsibility and authority.

The Informal Organization

In every organization there are two types of structures—the formal and the informal. Look for the "information centers" within the organization, the people who seem to know everything about what is going on. Even though a person may not hold a position of great responsibility, you may learn a great deal from him or her.

Fitting into Your Boss's Style

Your "boss" may be a committee, a congregation, or an individual. In any event, they will have their own way of doing things. Do some testing very early by bringing problems to them. See whether they expect you to make the decisions alone or whether they expect to be included in the decision-making process. If necessary, go out of your way to find reasons to place problems and decisions before them. In each case, you can ask the questions, "Is this the kind of a decision you'd like me to make alone?" or "Is this the kind of a problem that you would like to discuss with me or you'd like me to handle on my own?"

Stay Flexible

Remember that you're like a branch that has been broken off from a wild olive tree and grafted into a cultivated olive tree. The organization has probably been growing and going its own way. Now "new blood" is being brought in. Keep your goals clear, but keep your means flexible.

Be Patient

It is very common to overestimate what we can accomplish in one year and considerably underestimate what we can accomplish in five. Don't get discouraged when your first goals aren't realized as you planned. You will constantly need to set goals and reset them. Be patient and you will be surprised at the results.

:06

How to Get Control of Your Job

The Christian leader works with people power, money, experience, information and time. A failure in any one of these five areas will usually keep you from performing adequately. The most important of these is time. People power can be engaged, resources can be raised, experience can be developed, information can be gained, but time is not a variable.

To be a good manager we must gain control of our position. The first sign of control is when we sense that we are *managing our time*. As we said earlier, with references to the job, there are four kinds of time: superior time (demanded by your leaders); peer time (required by those with whom you work); subordinate time (demanded by those who work for you); and discretionary time (that remaining in your direct control). When you sense you have a balance between these, this is the first sign that you are beginning to get control.

The second sign that you are gaining control is when you feel you have *adequate information* to carry out your task. Note that we say adequate. You will never have enough information. But somewhere along in the process you should make some projections as to the kind of information you will need and set some goals for obtaining it. Then you will be prepared to accomplish your task.

The third sign of control will be when you sense you have *enough experience* to carry out your task. Again, you'll never have enough experience. But there comes a time when you begin to believe that you now have been through enough of the routines and processes to manage the job.

31

The fourth sign that you are gaining control is you feel you have *enough resources* to carry out your job. Finally, the fifth sign of control is that you have *enough people power*. In many ways these last two are the easiest to acquire. However, if they do not exist in the organization, you will never be able to carry out your job effectively, so treat them with respect.

Look at Your Goals

These are just signs. The real evidence is that you are achieving goals. Of course, this assumes that in the very beginning of the job you staked out some goals for yourself and for the organization, and made them known to the degree that they needed to be advertised. You must frequently evaluate your progress and see to it that some of these goals are now past events; they have been accomplished; you are moving on to new things.

See It As a Process

At the end of your first month sit down and write some goals for the next three, six and twelve months. These should be goals for yourself, for the part of the organization which you control, and for the total organization. Use these goals to review with your superiors, peers and subordinates what you believe needs to be done. Have them tell you what they believe needs to be done.

One very good question you could use when talking to old-timers in the organization is, "What questions should I have asked you that I haven't asked?" Many times this will elicit all kinds of information that you may not be able to get in other ways.

It is essential that you keep *communicating* upward, sideward, and downward. One of the most overlooked causes of failure is that people don't communicate. They don't tell one another where they are and where they hope to go. This is particularly true in the Christian organization, where volunteerism is a major component. Many times the expectations of the members are greatly different from the expectations of the leadership. Effective communication can help prevent people from being offended or exploited.

Start with the Basics

Something *very* basic to good management is a *job description*. If you don't have one, you should! If the organization has never used job descriptions, then do the best you can to write your own and review it with those to whom you report.

If the organization does not have an *organizational chart*, make one. Who reports to you? To whom do you report? Such a chart is useful to show lines of authority and responsibility.

One way to picture the situation at a deeper level is to first ask the question, "To whom do I *relate*?" Then take a blank piece of paper. Draw a circle in the middle. Put your name in that circle. Now draw circles for individuals who are grouped all around you. Draw an arrow from you to them if you need to relate to them and an arrow from them to you if they need to relate to you. Many times both are needed.

Take this same diagram and draw a dotted line to all the people and groups who are dependent on you for their "success." Do the same for yourself: on whom are you dependent for success? Use whatever definition you want of "success." This will help you realize that in order for an organization to operate effectively, the people must be aware that what they have an impact on others.

Finally, let us remind you of the most basic contribution to successful management—prayer. Don't let Christian piety become so routine that you fail to base your *life* on it! Let's remember Christ's own words, "Apart from me you can do nothing."

:07

How to Make It Through the Day

It's everybody's problem, isn't it? For one person it is a question of "How am I ever going to get all of this done?" For another person it is wondering how he or she will handle the constant interruptions. For a smaller number of people it is a question of just not enjoying the work that is in front of them.

It's All Right Not to Finish

There is a sign over one of the desks in our office that says "A Clean Desk Is the Sign of a Disturbed Mind." You don't have to finish everything every day. It is interesting how people differ in this respect. Some people worry if there is nothing left to do at the end of the day. They wonder if they are going to have a job the next day. Other people feel like they are real failures if they haven't accomplished everything. They go home worrying about the next day's work. Find out what your style is. But remember, if we are part of an organization that is doing an effective and God-honoring task, there will probably always be more work to do.

Divide and Conquer

Make a list of the different things you are supposed to do and the goals you are trying to accomplish. Divide the list up into: 1) things that have to be done every day; 2) things that have to be done every few days, 3) things that have to be done once a week, and 4) things that have to be done less often. Make a rough estimate of how long it will take for each of these to be accomplished. Then you can determine when to begin each and when you should complete it.

It might also be a good idea to prioritize these different kinds of tasks. Which ones are very important, of high value? Assign these an "A." Which are somewhat important, of medium

35

value? Assign these a "B." That means that all the rest are not so important, of low value. Give them a "C." Share your priorities with your boss to make sure you are in agreement.

The Things-to-Do List

There probably is no more powerful organizer and tension reliever than the "Things-to-Do" list. If you spend the first 10 to 15 minutes of each day (or it could be 15 minutes in the evening) writing down all the things that have to be done in the day ahead, this helps to reduce your anxiety and eliminate the question, "What do I have to do next?" Some people like to prioritize such a list using the ABC technique so they can start with the most important things first. Other people take the activities from the list and fit them into their standard day.

How About a Daily Planner?

If you really want to get organized, a daily planning sheet is essential. Ones that list all of your appointments, as well as record your "things-to-do" under categories such as mail, telephone calls (with numbers), things to plan, things to acquire and so forth, are extremely helpful. You can buy some of these at stationery stores or design your own.

Plan for the Gaps

Every so often we get the reverse of an interruption. We suddenly "run out of work." We haven't really, of course. What has actually happened is that we have not planned far enough ahead. We haven't planned for just this kind of a situation. If you know, for instance, that it is worth your while to do filing when you have an extra 20 minutes, then use those gaps for filing. If there is reading that you need to do but it's not immediately important, keep it handy in a reading file near your desk. How about a prayer list? Maybe the Lord gave you that gap so that you could address Him specifically about some of the needs you have, or that others have, or just to praise Him.

A Work Log Helps

If you have a diverse work schedule, particularly if you are getting work from different quarters, you will find it very useful to keep a work log. It does not have to be complicated. Note the item, the name of the item, the person it is for, when you received it, when you promised it, when you began work on it and when you completed it. This will not only help you keep track of things, but it's a great asset if you're sick or unable to come in to the office and other people need to find out what needs to be done.

Experience also contributes to being a good manager. And the way to get experience is to decide how to do your task better, and begin. Now.

:08

Where Do You Get Authority?

Bill watched as Joe gave instructions to a clerk at a nearby desk. "Where does he get the right to tell her to do that?" he wondered.

In the next office Mary Andrews was concluding a discussion with her supervisor: "All right, Mr. Armstrong. If that is the way you want it, we'll do it that way. It's your decision."

Upstairs, President Block was finishing a phone call: "I'm sorry, Mr. Mayor, but I don't think my board of directors would let me do that."

All of these conversations deal with authority.

What Is Authority?

Authority has been defined in many ways. One that many find appealing is "the freedom or right to take action." Some perceive it as the right to initiate an action. The second definition helps us to understand that how we act is always based on what we perceive to be a situation. Our superior may believe that we have a great deal of authority, but if we don't perceive it in the same way, our ability to act will be limited.

By the above definitions everyone has some authority. Research has shown that in most organizations, every member believed they had some authority.

Where Does It Come From?

Authority is both delegated downward and awarded upward in an organization. When we speak of the authority that is present within an organization made up of volunteers, we must realize that those who accept a subordinate role, by virtue of that acceptance, delegated a portion of their authority (freedom) to their superiors. This is true even in an ecclesiastical structure.

The church has no authority over us that we are not willing to give it. True, we may believe that it should and does have authority. But in the end, that authority is based upon the summation of our individual beliefs, our action on them, and our willingness to submit to that authority.

The Authority of Position In an organization, there is first the ideal *authority of position*. We say "ideal," because, as we will discuss below, authority—the freedom or right to take action—is given in a number of other ways. But, starting with the formal organization, we see "lines of authority" that begin with the senior executive in the organization and then move down through the organizational hierarchy. It is assumed that the chief executive has the final authority ("The buck stops here.") and that he or she and the organization have delegated part of the authority to take action to others down the ladder. It is important to recognize that we delegate to a position. Too often we forget that a position is not just a person or a role. A position in an organization assumes responsibility for work. Organizations are purposeful. They are brought into being to accomplish something. Positions are organized to divide up the task for the intended purpose. The responsibility of a position is to accomplish the work that is expected of that position.

When Authority Is Given There is an implied or stated contract: "If you will commit yourself to accomplish this goal I (we) will delegate to you the authority necessary to achieve it." If this is not clearly seen, then the limits of authority will be fuzzy at best. The other side of the coin is that authority must be commensurate with responsibility. A leader can never give away all of his or her authority. That would be abdication. But, delegation must include enough authority for the person to act appropriately.

Other Sources of Authority We stated above that authority is both given and received. Often people will give others the authority to act or to lead, even though they are not subordinate to them in the organization. They may do this because of that person's reputation, experience, or expertise.

There is the authority *reputation*. If a person within the organization is known to have accomplished a great deal or as a person who can be trusted, then that person will have a degree of authority—freedom to initiate action—that may far exceed his or her position. People who have been with the organization for a long time, individuals who have held a previous office in a volunteer organization, or someone who has come from a recognized position in another company, all will be given a great deal of authority.

There is the authority of *experience.* If others believe that someone has considerable experience in a particular area, and has faced this type of a situation in the past and met it successfully, they are likely to delegate the authority to that person to make a final decision or to take leadership. That is why we often give considerable authority to the outside consultant whom we hope has dealt with problems like ours before.

Finally authority of *expertise,* or technical knowledge. This is closely related to the authority of experience. We live in a day where we depend on a great many experts. Often the person with the expertise is not the person who is in the "position" of authority. However, because of this person's perceived expertise, their opinion on a given matter is likely to prevail.

As we stated above, in the organization made up primarily of volunteers, authority is first given when one agrees to an implied or stated contract at the time he or she joins the organization. Theoretically, the authority of the responsible person is complete: Within the limits of the position, whatever he or she says goes. But there are further limits on the ability of an individual to exercise authority over another.

First, *the individual must believe that it is in his or her own ultimate best interest.* Even though what is being asked may be well within the authority of the one asking, human beings will consciously or subconsciously evaluate the outcome in personal terms. They may be willing to pay a short-term penalty, such as having to work overtime, or putting aside their family life, but in the long run, if they come to believe what is being asked will be detrimental to them, they will withdraw or even find ways to circumvent the request.

Second, *the individual must believe that it is in the best interest of the group or the organization.* This is particularly true in a Christian organization where there is a common allegiance to a higher authority than the organization itself. But, it is also true in the secular organization. If a flightline sergeant doesn't want the airplanes to fly, the general can give all the orders he wants, but somehow the planes won't leave the ground.

Third, *the individual must have the ability to do what is asked.* The request may be reasonable. It may be well within the parameters of the position, but if the people being asked do not have the know-how, no amount of authority can get the work done. This speaks to the need for training, as well as careful selection of staff.

Fourth, *the individual must understand what is expected of him or her.* You have no authority if you are unable to communicate what it is that you want to happen. If I speak only French, and you speak only German, I will have great difficulty getting you to do what I wish. If my description of what is needed is faulty, you won't be able to carry out my instructions either. Take the time to make sure that all instructions are understood as they are intended.

How Is Authority Established?

Authority should first be given to a position, but it should always be given on the *basis of a plan.* A statement of what is to be accomplished, how it is to be accomplished, and when it is to be accomplished, is necessary.

The best way for this to happen is for the superior and subordinate to agree on the objective or goal(s) to be accomplished. Then the superior should request a written plan as to how the objective is to be reached. This becomes a written proposal that can then be worked over until there is agreement between the two. At this point the plan becomes a contract, and authority is given to carry out the plan.

Most positions will have a number of major tasks and objectives for which the position is responsible. Each of these tasks needs a specific plan.

When authority is given on this basis, it centers where it should, on the work to be done, the goals to be reached, rather than on the authority of the person.

Authority in Christian Organizations

To what extent does the Christian leader's authority reach beyond the employer/employee relationship suggested by the implied contract we discussed above? Answers are important, but not easy. The authority of the leaders in a local church will be dependent upon the church's ecclesiology. The authority in the parachurch organization, such as a mission agency, will depend on how it was initially constructed. Some organizations view all their staff as "members." These members actually elect the leadership. Other Christian organizations are controlled by a board of directors that hires or dismisses the chief executive officer and then leaves the rest to him or her.

Regardless of what kind of internal relationship exists, it would be our opinion that once the offices have been filled, authority should be defined as we have outlined above. In other words, the position should be defined in terms of the work to be performed, and the authority of the position should be respected.

The Bible describes the church as fitted together like a human body, with each person having a special and important function. Each part must, in some sense, submit to the other parts, and give them the authority to carry out their roles. This submitting to one another is what authority is all about. It is given for the good of the whole, not for the exaltation of an individual. If the body is to act in a harmonious and purposeful way, then it is important that the authority—the freedom or right to take action—of each part be understood by each person.

**The
Beauty
of
the
Organization**

:09

Competence

competent *adj.* 1) having requisite ability or qualities; fit 2) rightfully belonging; proper 3) legally qualified or capable (SYN. see ABLE, SUFFICIENT).

Why is it that Christian organizations are so often characterized as long on spirituality and short on competence? If there is both a right way and a wrong way, Christian organizations and churches are seldom known as those who do things the *right* way. Opinions such as these are formed many times at an emotional level, perhaps unfairly, but they reflect a general attitude which we need to face head on.

Why Incompetence?

We have many excuses. Probably the most common one used by churches is, "What can you expect from a volunteer organization?" But even those organizations which have full-time career staffs are often accused of the same incompetence.

Another excuse we hear all too often is, "We just can't afford the best people. What can you expect for the salaries we pay?"

And then there are some old proverbs such as, "If it is worth doing, it is worth doing poorly." (Assuming that if one can't do it well, it still ought to be done.)

Competence Has to Do with People

An organization can be competent, but if it is, it is because the people within the organization are competent. As we will note below, organizations can develop right ways of doing things, ways which can be handed down from person to person. But even knowing how to do something the right way is not

43

Competence   adequate if the individual to whom the task is given cannot carry out the task. A major part of the Christian manager's job is to find the right people and match them to the tasks at hand. Management is all about people. Management has been defined as the art or science of getting work done through people. But management is not just getting people to do things. It is helping people to become things.

More Than the Sum of the Parts

On the surface, an organization is the sum of its members. Yet the genius of the organization is synergistic, the total equals more than the sum. The biblical model is to always see people in relationship to one another. Christians are told that we are specifically gifted to fit together, much like a human body (Eph. 4:16 and Rom. 12:4–5). Indeed, the Bible has a great deal to say about how the local church builds itself up when all the parts do their particular work. Anyone who has had a sore arm has a working illustration of what happens when part of the body is not competent.

The competent organization, like the church, needs to build itself up. This means that the individuals are working for the good of the whole. One of the joys of work is working together for a common purpose.

Competence Is Not Competitive

Note the first definition of competent. One of the synonyms is *fit*. The competent person is one who fits the job and fits within the organization. We talk about people who are overqualified or underqualified. Basically what we are saying is they are not competent (underqualified) or that they are competent for a job which requires more responsibility than they are given. Therefore, competence has no sense of competitiveness. It is not a question of whether I am intrinsically more competent than you. It is only when we ask the question, "Competent to do what?" that we begin to have comparisons.

Competence therefore can only be defined against what has to be done, what is to be accomplished.

Areas of Competency

From an organizational standpoint, there are fundamentally two kinds of work: *management work* and *technical work*. Management work includes planning, organizing, leading and controlling, all of which have to do with accomplishing work through others. Technical work has to do with specific areas such as finance, communication, typing, computer programming, etc. The Christian organization, however, adds a third dimension to these which, for lack of another definition, we will call spiritual competence. This is a difficult area to get a handle on and yet a very important one.

44

We are accustomed to talking about new Christians as those *Competence* who are "young in the faith" or "babes in Christ" or "spiritually immature." We are usually careful not to put such people in positions of spiritual leadership. It follows that we should expect levels of spiritual maturity to match levels of organizational leadership. It may be all right to have a young Christian working in a technical job where there is no need to supervise or manage people. But it is dangerous to put immature Christians in roles where they not only have to give spiritual counsel but make decisions requiring a depth of prayer and a strong biblical basis for what is right, good, and appropriate.

People grow. Organizations grow. People change. Organiza- **Competence** tions change. A major task of the manager is to continually ask, **Is** "Is this the right person for this job?" and "Is this the right job for **Not** this person?" The first question is an organizational one. Again **a** using the analogy of the body, an elbow that has grown out of **Static** proportion to the arm and the rest of the body is more likely to **Thing** hinder than to help. A wrist that doesn't have the strength to work with a hand leaves both incompetent.

The second question has to do with the individual. Often we hold on to people for the very reason that they are competent even when they have grown beyond the job and could do much more. This is not only bad for the person, but eventually will distort the body. If there is not a place for a person's growing skills and maturity to serve an organization, the Christian manager should help that person find a better place to serve God in His economy.

When building a competent staff one must follow some basic **How** guidelines. **Do**
1) *Purpose*: You can't decide what kind of people you need **We** until you have clearly defined the fundamental purpose of your **Get** organization. **Competent**
2) *Objectives*: There are some long range things that your **People?** organization must do if it is to fulfill its purpose. What are they? This is the major weakness of most not-for-profit organizations, churches and parachurch groups. Christians are future-oriented people. We believe that somehow God intends to use us to carry out His purposes. But we have to decide specifically what it is we are to accomplish.
3) *Structure*: Our organizational structure should reflect our objectives. It will indicate to us the natural formations and work groupings. When is the last time you sat down with your organi- 45 zational chart in front of you and asked, "Does this structure make sense in light of what we are trying to accomplish?"

4) *Position Description*: The trouble with most position or job descriptions is that they describe things like "responsibilities" and "accountability." That's fine. We need those things defined. But the primary purpose of a position description or position charter should be to describe the objectives of the individual working in this area. The higher up we move in the organization, the more important this becomes. What does this position description tell you about the skills and gifts the position needs?

5) *Selection*: The biggest failure in selecting people is not taking the time to get that *fit* which is part of our definition of competence. There is an interesting psychological factor at work here. Often we find someone who at first glance looks just right. We spend time and effort learning about this person, talking with him or her, perhaps even doing some convincing about why this person should work with us. About the time we are ready to make a formal invitation, some clouds appear on the horizon. We see some areas of weakness. But we have invested so much of our time and emotional energy, that we go ahead and hire the person anyway, hoping for the best. It takes a great deal of energy, and often a lot of courage, to keep working until we find the competent person.

6) *Standards*: Most people will respond to the expectations of their leaders. If the leader has high expectations of the person, so will that person. If the leader doesn't expect much, chances are that person won't either. Expectations are communicated through standards, descriptions of what is to be done and how to do it. This is one of the most difficult managerial tasks. Good performance needs to be reinforced. Less than adequate performance needs to be pointed out, and steps need to be given for its improvement. It takes time. It takes a competent manager!

7) *Delegation*: This is really the other side of the standards coin. If delegation is assigning work to people and management is accomplishing results through others, they are not much different. Delegation assumes that part of the work can be done more effectively by someone other than the delegator. It assumes that the one receiving the delegation is competent to do the task delegated. Delegation takes a lot of time. It often seems easier to do a task ourselves, rather than ask someone else to do it. But when we fail to delegate, we are in effect working at a level less than our own competency, while depriving someone who is competent the opportunity to do what they do well.

8) *Training*: This is talked about a lot, isn't it? But somehow it seems like it either costs too much or we don't have the time. Gifts need to be sharpened into skills. As the nature of the work expands, the people must also expand. It is interesting how

many churches will give training in evangelistic follow-up counseling, but fail to train ushers, hospital visitors, committee chairpersons—you name it.

Perhaps you believe that in some special mysterious way God has placed you in the position you are in. But that is not enough. You must evaluate your competency in that role. Growth requires a constant review of what we can do and what we need to learn to do. Competent leaders/managers can seldom do all the things they ask others to do. That's what delegation is all about. Therefore the competent leader will recognize the need to find competent people.

:10:

Integrity

---

integrity *n*. 1) an unimpaired condition; soundness 2) firm adherence to a code of esp. moral or artistic values; incorruptibility 3) the
quality or state of being complete or undivided: completeness (SYN.
see HONESTY, UNITY).

Integrity is doing what you said you would do. It is fundamental to all sound management. It is a mixture of both doing
what is right and what is expected.

Doing What Is Expected

Promise keeping is the bedrock of social relationships. When
we can no longer depend on one another to do what we said we
will do, the future becomes an undefined nightmare.

Society makes promises to us. Governments make promises
to us. Our friends make promises. The church makes promises.
All of these have to do with the future. Each one says, "When
the time comes, you can depend on me to do this," or "This will
happen." The most fundamental and mysterious promises are
those made between a man and woman in the act of marriage.
Here is a promise which essentially says, "Forever."

No organization can operate for very long if people do not do
what they say (promise) they will do. All management systems
are based on promise keeping. "Management by objectives"
assumes that each person will achieve the goal to which he or
she is committed, or will give early notice to the possibility of
nonperformance. "Management by Exception" assumes that
the management is really interested in those objectives and
promises that are not being kept.

49

Few of us think of the commitments we make in the organizational setting as promises. For most of us a promise is something we make to the Lord, to ourselves or to a loved one. A promise seems to have much more moral value than a written work objective. But one of the highest compliments you can give to an organization as well as to an individual is: "They keep their commitments. They do what they say they will." How else could we say it?: "They have integrity."

Promises within the Organization

The Cornerstone of Management

Integrity—soundness, incorruptibility, completeness—is the cornerstone of any structure. It begins with the technical aspects of our work, those things that don't (appear to) have moral value, and then includes the values that control who we are and what we do.

The announcement of a Mission Emphasis Week in our church is a promise to the congregation that 1) we are interested in missions, and 2) if you set aside the time, we will provide a program which will benefit you and others.

When an organization sets fundraising goals, it is stating its intention to provide funds for whatever its ministry will be. There is an implied commitment that 1) we believe this is possible and desirable, and 2) we are going to do what has to be done to see it happen.

When a department head promises an analysis of a problem to an executive director by next Tuesday, she has made the same statement: 1) I believe it can be done, and 2) I will do it.

When a church board member accepts a position, the same two commitments are implied.

In every case there is an understanding that we will do what we said we will do.

But It Doesn't Always Work That Way

All promises have to do with the future. None of us can control or accurately predict the future. And the further into the future we are promising, the higher the probability something unforeseen will happen to upset our plans. So there is a third commitment implied in setting a goal or making a promise: 3) I will tell you as soon as I doubt my ability to keep my commitment or promise. Integrity will be maintained. I will not let you go along believing we are still on course if we are not.

This is why all the planning we do needs to be balanced by the controls that help us know, in a reasonably routine way, how we are doing. Activity reports, planning reviews, weekly meetings should be designed as opportunities to communicate with one another.

How different it sounds when instead of talking about review-

ing plans and objectives, we picture ourselves as reviewing the
promises we have made and making new ones.

We will make mistakes. Things will go wrong. The unexpected will happen. If everyone is to learn from all of this, and if we are to keep faith in one another, there must also be a fourth step: 4) I will tell you why I believe I was unable to keep my commitment and what I am going to do about it in the future.

To sum up what has been said, people who have integrity are **Four** those who: **Steps**

1) Set goals (make promises) for themselves and their organi-**in** zations which they believe can be accomplished. **Promise**

2) Put all of their energy into doing what they said they would **Keeping** do.

3) Tell those to whom they have committed when they believe they are no longer able to keep their commitment.

4) Attempt to understand the reason for failure and what corrective action they will need to take in the future.

The same can be said for organizations, including the local church.

Notice that if there are no commitments or promises, it will **Learning** be very difficult to develop a reputation for integrity. One has to **Integrity** practice integrity.

Practicing integrity is a two-way street. If I make a commitment to you, you need to hold me to my commitment. If I said I would do it (either as an individual or as a unit within the organization), and the time comes when you believe I haven't done it, you need to ask me about it.

If you don't ask, I can conclude a number of things: Perhaps you don't care. Perhaps you are so busy that you are not keeping your commitment to me as my leader. Perhaps the thing I have committed to really isn't important.

On the other hand, if you do hold me accountable there are some other things I may learn: You expect me to do what I said I would. Keeping my commitments is important. What I am doing is important enough so that if it is not done, the organization will suffer. I am important enough so that if I don't keep my commitments, the organization will be hurt.

If often costs a great deal to maintain integrity, to keep our commitments. Sometimes it may cost the organization a great deal to do something just because we said we would. Many times it is easy to conclude that we had better let this one slip because the extra expense involved will really stress us. When 51 that happens, we lose some of our integrity.

**The
Moral
Side
of
Integrity**

So far we have dealt with what might be called "value-free" integrity. On the surface, it appears that whether a report was written on time or whether a shipment of supplies was one week late, is not a moral issue. However, to make a promise is a holy thing. I am committing a part of my life to you when I make a promise. I am announcing that you have an interest in my future. I am stating that you can expect your life to go as you would hope because of my willingness to fit into your needs and desires. The good and faithful servant was placed as a ruler over five cities because he had been faithful in smaller things. He had demonstrated integrity. You could count on him to do what he committed himself to do.

The same thing is true about organizations. The Bible describes the relationships that exist within the church as analogous to the various parts of the body. Each part has not only been fitted to make the body sound and complete, but is also expected to perform as expected.

**Let's
Not
Promise
Too
Much**

One of the biggest traps many of us fall into is making too many promises at one time. When we say we can do something, we are also saying we have the time to do it. It is important to make commitments and follow through on them, but we must be aware of our available time before accepting too many. Somehow it is just as wrong when someone says, "I wanted to do what I promised, but I didn't have the time" as when they say, "I just didn't feel like doing it."

Integrity is keeping promises—doing what you said you would do.

·11

How to Light a Fire under People without Burning Them Up

"Why can't I get Betty to finish the curtains she promised for the Sunday school room?"

"Whatever happened to Bill? He was gung ho on this project six months ago, and now he never turns up for meetings."

"Pastor, I'd love to see that job done, but nobody around here wants to do anything."

Are these typical of some of the things you have heard lately? What's going on? Does it seem like the "good old days" when everyone pitched in are long past? How do you light a fire under people to get them moving? And how do you light a fire under people without burning them up? How do you *motivate* people?

The answers to these questions are not simple. The fact is, it is very difficult to motivate people. But there is a better way; find people who are already motivated.

Let's assume that you're a leader of a local church or some other kind of organization, perhaps a volunteer one. Where do you begin, and what can you do that will strengthen the probability that you and your group will have a positive and God-honoring experience? Let's sum it up under three headings: 1) begin together, 2) build a group, and 3) keep motivating.

Begin Together

People are motivated by their own goals. Many people feel that, "Good goals are my goals and bad goals are your goals." Or as a group might put it, "Good goals are our goals and bad goals are their goals." It is important to begin any new program by seeking out those individuals who will already be attracted by the goals. How can we do this?

First, we need to recognize that not everyone will be either

53

motivated, equipped or called to a particular task. For example, everyone is called to be a witness, but not all are gifted as evangelists. If we attempt to enlist everyone in a program of evangelism, we will not only fail, but we will leave a lot of people with great feelings of guilt. So, don't expect that everyone will be interested. At the same time, don't mistake their lack of interest for antagonism.

The place to start is with a clear vision of what needs to happen and why it needs to happen. We want people to first get involved in identifying the problem that needs to be solved. Then we can work together to discover ways to solve it.

As you give assignments, take care to recognize the capability of people. Attempt to tailor the size of the task to the gifts of the people. Knowing your people is a crucial component of motivating them.

**Build
a
Group**

There are three key words: *delegation, accountability* and *communication.* As we will see, communication is both delegation and accountability.

Communication

Communication moves in four directions. First, you have to understand what needs to be done and continue to keep yourself informed. Second, you have to keep the people on your team informed. If the ushering committee is going to be a success, they need to know what you're thinking and what each of them is thinking. Third, you need to keep people on other teams and committees informed. It really isn't much fun to call a meeting for the ushering committee to go through a practice in the sanctuary only to discover that the choir has a special rehearsal the same night. Fourth, you have to keep the leaders of the organization informed. If you are going to continue to have their support, and if they are going to be able to function as leaders of the whole organization, they need to know.

Delegation

Delegation is the bugaboo of most volunteer organizations. People fear delegation for a number of reasons: First, they may be afraid they're going to be stuck with something "forever." You failed to put a time limit on the delegation. Second is the fear of failure; they feel the job is too big for them or too time-consuming.

Both these fears can be overcome if we realize that delegation comes at a number of different levels. Seldom are we asking someone to do something all by themselves without accountability to someone else. Therefore, we need to set limits on the amount of work we ask people to do. Communicate to them whether they are to do it by themselves, in consultation with

54

other people, or if they're just responsible to gather information and then report back.

The next issue which needs to be addressed is when the task will be completed. But knowing when is not going to be very helpful unless you know how you and the rest of the group will know it's done. Build reporting systems into the assignment at the time of planning. There are many ways to do this. One that many task groups in churches have found particularly helpful, is to write out a postcard for all of the things that are going to happen and then mail it to the responsible individual a week or ten days before the event. Ask them if everything is under control.

Accountability

We noted above that if people don't know how to do something, they can't very well do it. They need to be trained. If a local church had only one full-time pastor and was seeking an associate, we would heartily recommend a person whose only job was recruiting and training lay people. After all, the ministry is the work of the laity. The work of a pastor is to pastor, not administrate. If you are going to have an outstanding ushering team, if people are going to be pleased and proud of the way their ushering works, then you are going to have to train people how to be ushers.

Train to Do the Job

We've already said that it's very difficult to motivate people. People usually come already motivated. Some things motivate people, while others, although they won't motivate them, by their absence will demotivate them. People are motivated by achievement, by recognition of their efforts, by challenging work, by being made responsible, and by experiencing personal growth. People are demotivated by poor administration, weak supervision, bad working conditions, poor interpersonal relationships, and the absence of a feeling of status and security.

Keep Motivating

What is likely to motivate a good usher? *Achievement*—perhaps experienced by learning to do something that he or she has not known how to do before, and by doing it well. *Recognition*—perhaps by seeing his or her name in the church bulletin or by having the pastor recognize from the pulpit that the ushering staff is doing a good job. *Challenging work*—by giving them the opportunity to find ways to enhance the worship service in their church. *Responsibility*—by holding them accountable to do their job, and praising them for their faithfulness. *Personal growth*—by learning new things, and doing something worthwhile. For example, he or she may have initiated something

Motivators

55

like a Bible study among the other ushers which has contributed to his growth as well as that of others in the group.

There are several practical things the manager can do to motivate his or her staff:

1) *Recognize their effort.* If you see people obviously trying to do a good job, strengthen their efforts by pointing out to them that they are doing a good job, and you appreciate their diligence.

2) *Recognize their results.* When there has been a particularly effective worship service, let the ushering staff know that they have contributed to it. Recognize those who are on time for meetings. Recognize their efficiency. Verbal recognition and written recognition are both very motivating.

3) *Be committed to their ability.* If you, as the leader of the group, don't believe in them, who will? Let people know that you're committed to their ability to handle the tasks before them. Encourage them and be careful not to step in and do their tasks for them.

4) Finally, *don't compare people with people.* People should be compared to themselves. There will always be someone who can do the job better than the person who's doing it, but that person is not here and this person is. God has placed him here. You placed him or her here. Believe in people and trust in God.

Demotivators   Let's look at the demotivators: *Lack of administration*—a feeling that no one cares about the rest of the worship service, can quickly lead the ushering staff to feel as if their job is not important. *Poor supervision*—discovering that no one is checking to see if the job is done well, can quickly become demoralizing. *Poor working conditions*—for instance, having no place for the ushering staff to prepare for the service, or no place to count the money, can discourage them. *Poor interpersonal relationships*—if the members of the ushering staff are unable to get along well, some will eventually want to quit. *Lack of status and security*—feeling that the job is just not worthwhile and nobody appreciates it will demotivate people. Having good administration, good supervision, good working conditions, and even good interpersonal relationships, will not necessarily motivate people. But if these are absent demotivation is sure to occur.

How do you light a fire under people without burning them up? You let them help you build the fire and warm yourselves together in its glow.

12

Decision Making

Many years ago a Christian leader wrote a letter to some of his followers in Corinth reflecting back on his decision not to visit them: "Was I vacillating when I wanted to do this? Do I make my plans like a worldly man, ready to say yes and no at once? As surely as God is faithful, our word to you has not been yes and no. For the Son of God, Jesus Christ, whom we preached among you, Sylvanus, Timothy and I, was not yes and no; but in Him it is always yes."

Paul faced all the demands for making a decision. The situation demanded action. He was under time pressure. He lacked complete information. There was uncertainty which suggested a risk in making a decision. There were possible costly consequences if he made the wrong decision. On the other hand, there was the possibility of good benefits from an effective decision. Lastly, there was the possibility of two or more alternative actions.

Good decision making is the hallmark of effective leadership in an organization. But good decision making from a Christian perspective requires an additional dimension. It is this additional spiritual dimension that can give the Christian executive the confidence he needs to move ahead with a decision while others stand and vacillate.

There is a close relationship between decision making and problem solving. Usually both start with a statement like: "Something needs to be done!" The steps in the process are not difficult to describe: 57

1) *Identify and describe the situation.* Gather as many relative facts together as possible.

2) *Line up alternatives.* These may range from taking no action (a decision in itself), to a number of possible actions.

3) *Compare the various alternatives.* There will usually be advantages and disadvantages to each.

4) *Calculate the risk of each.* Since you usually will not have enough information to make a perfect decision, face up to the possible consequences of each alternative.

5) *Select the best alternative.* If alternatives have been adequately compared and rated as to risk, many times the best one will be self-evident.

Your first reaction may be that anything that complicated just isn't useful. But our mind is able to comprehend and digest so many things in a brief moment. The process by which comprehension occurred just takes longer to describe.

Describing the Situation

Many times our ability to understand a situation is half of the solution. Gather as many facts as possible. There will never be enough, but within the time demands of the decision, take time to organize the data that is available. When this is done, describe the situation as accurately as possible.

Data gathering is a skill that needs to be developed. Find out what the key sources of information are. Decide if others should be called in to contribute information. But remember that you're asking for data, not opinions on what decisions should be made.

Line Up Alternatives

From the data that you have gathered, list possible alternatives in a way that will permit you to visualize them all at one time. If you are working with a group, it is very helpful to write the data (problem description) on one piece of paper and then to list the alternatives on another.

There will be cases when the alternatives for a decision are either yes or no, go or don't go. However, try not to be satisfied with only two alternatives. Seek wise counsel. Ask several people for possible alternatives based upon the data that you have.

Compare the Alternatives

Since we can never completely predict the future, almost every alternative will include some factor of uncertainty. Find some way to compare alternatives. Some factors you might want to compare are: the *risk* involved (see below), the *cost* of the alternative, the *people available* to implement the decision, the *past effectiveness* of using this type of alternative, the *amount of time* that this alternative will require, and *how it will be received* within the organization.

58

A *list of assumptions* that you are making for each one of the alternatives may be a key to which is the best. It is surprising how often people arrive at the same conclusion for different reasons. Therefore, a side benefit of listing your assumptions is your ability to communicate to others (and yourself!) the base upon which you are building your reasoning.

How much time you take in this process will, of course, be dictated by the urgency of the decision you face.

Calculate the Risk

The major difference between problem solving and decision making is that in problem solving we assume there is a right solution. The problem has an answer. But decision making almost always includes an element of risk. We don't have enough information. We are not sure of the future. We don't have enough time to gather all the data. Therefore, try to develop your own method of rating the risk of each of the alternatives. Perhaps something as simple as a grading scale of 1 to 10 will be of help. Look back at your previous assumptions and see if they help you in assessing the penalties for making the wrong decision.

Many times the correct alternative is self-evident as we compare and rate the risk of each one of the various alternatives. But there are many times when it is very difficult to choose between alternatives. What do we do then?

Sometimes we can combine alternatives. This can be done by taking parts of two different alternatives or perhaps trying both of them. For instance, one might be a short-range solution to the need you face while the other might be a longer range solution. Don't be afraid of a compromise. Inflexibility in decision making tends to destroy effective leadership. Often all you can do is make the best out of a series of bad situations. Intuition or hunches will also play a major role in selecting the "best" alternatives. Here is where the spiritual dimension really matters. Pray about the alternatives. Seek God's promised wisdom.

Implement the Decision

Many times how a leadership decision is announced and implemented is just as important as the decision itself. If it will have a major impact on the life of the organization, consider the *timing* of the announcement. Perhaps it should be postponed until just the right set of circumstances present themselves. When you make an important decision, take a little time before announcing it. Sleep on it. God may have other plans!

The *manner* in which the decision is announced is of tremendous importance. If it is presented as "I'm sorry, fellows, but this is the best we can do in this lousy situation . . .", then you can expect the same response from your subordinates as they communicate the decision throughout the organization. 59

The *individuals* to whom the decision is announced can

make a big difference in its reception. Many times it is a good idea to privately lay some groundwork ahead of time with those who are going to have to implement a major decision or will be affected by it.

Once a decision is made, don't look back or second guess yourself. Expect and demand commitment to the decision, on your part, and on the part of those who are going to be working on it. Don't seek popularity in decision making. Leadership can be a lonely business. Be consistent in applying the consequences of your decision. Don't vacillate.

When Things Go Wrong

In the next chapter we will discuss Murphy's Law: "If there is a possibility of anything going wrong, it probably will." What may have been a very good decision three weeks ago, in the light of subsequent events or new data, may appear to be a very poor one. This means that important decisions should have a built-in feedback process which will let you know as soon as possible if things are going sour. At this point, it is not a question of who's at fault, but how to turn things in a more positive direction. In a sense, you are faced with a new decision: what to do with the bad one you've made! It may be that the decision was right, but the planning was poor. Perhaps the wrong individuals were given the assignment to implement. Perhaps a new and better alternative has appeared, one which is distracting people from the original course of action. Go through the same process of decision making you went through before: identify the situation, line up alternatives, compare alternatives, calculate the risk, select the best new alternative, implement a new and revised decision.

It is here that the Christian executive or church leader has the advantage over his or her secular counterpart. Each one of us as children of God can be assured that God is working all things together for good on our behalf. But those of us who are privileged to work as part of the organizational life of His Body have the right to assume that this applies equally to the organizational task. This does not mean that we should be casting blame for failure on the Lord. Nor should we discount our own role in any "successes." It does mean that that extra dimension can produce decisions which can turn the world upside down.

13

Murphy's Law

People have always attempted to make some sense out of God's universe. With the advent of Newtonian physics, we began to describe the world in terms of "laws," rules by which we could bring some consistency and predictability to life. We have learned the hard way that the "laws" of one generation often become the laughingstock of others. But still the search continues.

Perhaps the failure to find ongoing consistency in the material universe is what one day encouraged Mr. Murphy to postulate his now famous law: "If anything can go wrong, it probably will."

Think of all the possible failures. Consider all of the possible mistakes. They will happen, so says Mr. Murphy.

In more recent years a Mr. O'Toole has framed O'Toole's Comment on Murphy's Law: "Murphy was an optimist."

We suspect that Murphy was a young man when he framed his law (and O'Toole was even younger). For as we get older, we learn to accept the fact that not only will things go wrong, but there is much to be learned from such occasions.

Why is it that some people seem to get things done with ease and little fuss, while others apparently encounter nothing but failure? We suspect it has something to do with the age at which they learned Murphy's Law and began applying it to the storing up of "experience."

Why do things go wrong? It sounds overly simple but it boils down to when, where, what and how.

The desired event didn't happen when we needed it, or what

61

we wanted wasn't where we wanted it, or the thing that was produced was not what we wanted or we didn't know how to do it or did it incorrectly.

Why Things Go Wrong

From a management viewpoint there are two kinds of time: *elapsed time*, the time that goes by on the clock or the calendar, and *work time*, the time when we are actually engaged in work. We can seldom do an hour's work in an hour. During that hour there will usually be interruptions. Although the amount of time spent at the task (work time) may actually add up to only an hour, when we look at the clock, we discover the time allotted (elapsed time) has exceeded the hour.

Experience teaches us to leave room for the unexpected or to isolate ourselves in order to minimize interruptions.

Where Is It?

It's surprising how often the right thing manages to arrive in the wrong place. Shipments of material are held up. People who have needed skills are at another location. The "right" solution is applied to the wrong problem. All of the elements or parts needed are available, except for one. For example, preconference planning for a major consultation is complete, but someone forgot to ask whether there was a public address system available.

Experience anticipates the possibility and starts asking in time to correct the error. It remembers the things that went wrong before and makes checklists that others can follow.

What Do You Want?

How many times have you ordered something only to have something else delivered? How often are you faced with, "Oh, I thought you meant. . ."? The task gets done, but it has the wrong outcome. Murphy's Law strikes again.

Experience tells us that we can't be certain someone really understands until they are able to explain to us what we said. The best plans are not the ones we create, but the ones that others create and the leader approves.

How Do You Do It?

How one does something has to do with procedures and methods. This is where we find "human error." Most of us think of applying Murphy's Law in this area. Interestingly, human error is the easiest kind of problem to overcome. If you know what it is you want to accomplish, and you know how long it will take, chances are great that you can find someone with the adequate skills to accomplish it.

Experience knows that resources, such as money or people, are part of the solution, not the problem.

An Italian economist by the name of Pareto observed some time ago that 80 percent of life's problems are caused by 20 percent of life's events. Salesmen find they get 80 percent of their orders from 20 percent of their customers. Managers discover that they need to spend 80 percent of their time on 20 percent of their problems. Pastors may discover they spend 80 percent of their time with 20 percent of their parishioners.

Murphy's Law helps us to recognize that something can go wrong with almost anything, but it does not follow that everything will go wrong all of the time. In fact, a little reflection will cause us to see that we are all used to living with a great deal of "failure" each day. We accept the fact that the greatest baseball player of all time batted only .400. (He "failed" six times out of ten!) We leave ourselves enough time to get to work, recognizing that we might get caught in a traffic jam.

If we live in a world where anything can go wrong, and if Pareto is right that 20 percent of the "failures" will consume 80 percent of our time, then it follows that what we need to do is to identify the disastrous 20 percent.

The task for the executive is to know what 20 percent to focus on. Another name for such an approach is "Management by Exception." Don't be concerned about the things that are going well. Look for the weak points.

But how does one do this? The answer lies not only in hundreds of books on management practice and theory, but in a good deal of experience (!) that has to be lived. But there is a simple outline of steps that perhaps will increase the chance of discovering the key 20 percent. It follows the same outline as the problem: when, where, what and how. They are questions which need to be asked when we plan, when we evaluate, and when we replan.

The next time you have to estimate the amount of time needed to prepare for a sermon, design a program, or carry out a task, begin by asking (yourself or the person responsible), "How long will it take?" Write down the answer. Next ask, "What's the fastest we could possibly do it?" Write that down. Finally ask, "If everything goes wrong, how long will it take?" Write that down.

When you analyze the three answers, chances are that your original time estimate will be more optimistic or pessimistic than the final one. Use your best judgment to decide which is the best guess. Keep track of how long each part of the task takes.

You'll discover one usually takes longer. You now know the Pareto 20 percent for the *time* dimension.

Where Will It Be?

The "where" question is usually applicable to only part of a task. It assumes that you are faced with a problem of geography. Find those things that have to come the furthest distance, either in number of stops or actual miles. For example, a special printing job being done by an out-of-town contractor. Those are the 20 percent for "where?"

What Do You Want?

Letting others know what you want is a matter of clear communication. What individual or organization is least likely to understand what you have asked for? For example, making arrangements in a country that has few English speakers, or dealing with people you have never met can be a potential problem. These are Pareto's 20 percent.

How Do You Do It?

One of the advantages of spending a lot of time planning is that you can look at a number of alternative ways of doing things, and select those that are optimum for your task. If you discover in your planning that there is only one way to do something, there is no other alternative, that's your 20 percent. For if that one fails, you have no way out until you do find an alternative.

How dull a life it would be if everything happened as anticipated! How wonderful to know that God can take our "mistakes" and work them out for good. Joseph must have certainly felt that Murphy had been around! His brothers sold him as a slave. His master's wife tried to seduce him. Those he befriended in prison forgot him. We can learn from Joseph's response to his brothers: "You meant it for evil, but the Lord meant it for good."

Dayton's Law

Ed Dayton would like to suggest a new "law" which hereafter will be known as Dayton's Law: "At least 50 percent of the things you plan will probably go right. Rejoice."

:|4

On Taking Risks

In responding to the generosity of the Philippian church and their concern for his welfare, Paul commends to them their brother Epaphroditus: "Welcome him in the Lord with great joy, and honor men like him, because he almost died for the work of Christ, risking his life to make up for the help you could not give me" (Phil. 2:29–30, NIV). Most of us are not called upon to put our lives at risk in the everydayness of our Christian service. On the other hand, most of us would probably be uncomfortable with the thought that we were not willing "to risk all for Christ."

But what about risk when it comes to leading the organization? It is one thing to personally risk our life or our fortune or our reputation. But what about risking the life, the fortune or the reputation of the organization we lead?

The authors have long since given up the idea that there are **It** standard answers for life's situations. The world refuses to fit **All** into our categories. In a real sense the Bible is not an answer **Depends** book, but a question book. Asking the right question within the context of the situation is usually the most important thing we can do.

With that in mind, we immediately recognize that there are some people who appear to take too many risks and others who appear to take too few. How do we find the middle ground? What are the questions?

There is a truism which says that organizations are started by a *man* (or woman), and during their beginnings they reflect that

**Man,
Movement,
Machine,
Monument**

person and his or her life and world view. If they progress, they become a *movement*. Others are caught up in the directions they are moving. But movements tend to become *machines*. They tend toward order, discipline, rules and regulations, all of which can make them quite machine-like. When that happens, the organization can become nothing more than a *monument* to those who began it. In the beginning there was someone who was willing to risk everything to make something happen. In the end there was no one who was willing to risk anything.

It is a fact of life that one of the characteristics of the "natural leader" or entrepreneur is a willingness to take risk. It is also true that managers, particularly middle managers, tend to avoid risk.

Where do we find a balance?

**Who's
in
Charge
Here?**

Most organizations are about the business of *getting things done*. After all, there is a "bottom line" out there! We have work to do!

True. But the Christian counterbalance to the task of doing God's work, is the recognition that it is God who is doing the work. He is the One who has prepared all the good works we are going to do (Eph. 2:10). And He will get it done (in spite of us!). Our local church may disappear from its corner next week. Our high-powered, dynamic Christian enterprise may fail tomorrow. God's work will get done.

Another need for finding balance.

**A
Lot
of
Life
Is
Failure**

Some say that a lot of life is failure. That sounds like a pretty crass statement, doesn't it? But let's examine it a little. Ted Williams, one of the greatest hitters of all time in American baseball, set a record by hitting the ball four times out of ten when he was at bat. But the other side of that coin is that he missed, he failed, six times out of ten.

How did he become such a good batter? By learning to overcome the mistakes he made when he was not such a good hitter.

Our life situations are similar. Living life is like driving a car. We keep looking out through the windshield of life at the world rushing at us, correcting here, and compensating there. Roads get blocked. We take detours. Tires go flat. Cars need servicing. But we go on. And in the driving there is always the risk that someone else won't stop at the intersection, or for just a moment our attention may be diverted. Both driving and living involve taking risks.

66

It is not a question of whether we will take risks. Rather, it is a question of which risks to take. To do nothing may be the riskiest thing we can do. The one thing we can be certain ot is change, and it hurts to change. It's risky to change.

How then does the organization decide which risks to take? The answer is simple to state and difficult to carry out: Have an extensive program of strategic (or long-range) planning.

Planning is not intended to avoid risk. One way to define planning is "risk taking—decision making." To make plans is to make decisions now that will have an impact on us tomorrow. When we decide, we put the organization at risk.

Perhaps you have never thought about it that way. Perhaps you never realized that when you made plans you were "risking" the organization. But that's a healthy way to think about it. It calls us to consider the consequences of our decisions. It asks the question, "Which is the lesser risk for the desired gain?"

Statistical theory has a concept known as "confidence limits." Confidence limits recognize that in dealing with probabilities we can seldom be 100 percent certain. Therefore, it has developed a way of telling the person interested how likely it is that the data presented represents reality. In its simplest form we hear statements like, "There is a 60 percent probability of rain tomorrow." We hear results of the Gallup poll that may talk about, "The margin of error for these statements is five percent." To put that another way, we can say that we are 95 percent confident that the data is what it says it is.

Now let's apply that to long-range planning and risk taking. What confidence limits do we want to place on a given plan or suggestion for the future? Let's use a fundraising example: What confidence do we have that the suggested program will have the desired result?

We will immediately discover that the answers tend to be quite subjective. Someone may say, "How would I know whether it's 50 percent or 75 percent?" You may not. But you evidently know that it is not 10 percent, nor is it 95 percent. When one begins to compare different possibilities, these relatively crude numbers give us helpful insight.

So our first question was, "What is the probability that this program will produce the desired result?" That can break down into two subquestions: 1) What is the probability that we can do what we say we will? and, 2) What is the probability that if the program works, it will produce the intended result?

Again, to use the fundraising example—if our plan to increase the number of contributors to our organization by 20 percent is successful, will that in turn produce the needed income?

The next question of cost-benefit analysis is one that is familiar to most of us: Is the cost of doing the program worth the intended result? Change always has costs. Are we ready for them?

**The
Other
Side
of
the
Coin**

When we have answered these questions, we are ready to look at the risks involved in various programs in a positive way.

But first there is a negative question: For each of the possible approaches, what is the cost of failure, of not achieving the announced result? This question not only helps us choose the program with the least risk for the desired benefit, but it also gives us some clues as to what to do if indeed the program does fail. We need to plan for both success and failure.

A basic element of any planning should therefore be a comparison of the alternatives with some confidence limits on the probability of success for each major program and, an analysis of the consequences of only partial success or failure.

**Courage
Is
Knowing**

The future is never certain. It can be only hoped for at best. The further into the future we move the consequences of our actions and the longer range our planning, the less likelihood there is that we will be accurate. It takes courage to look at the future. It takes even more courage to risk making decisions in the face of an uncertain future where the dangers of failure are known. (It takes little courage to face a future of unknown consequences.)

That is why it takes courage to be a good leader. The effective leader accepts the fact that the future is unknown, attempts to reduce uncertainty by choosing between a number of alternatives, makes a decision and then takes the risk to move out.

**The
Christian
Edge**

In a world where Christ is rarely acknowledged, taking risks can be a gut-rending experience. It's not pleasant to contemplate the results of a bad major decision. One's entire career or future may be riding on the outcome.

This is also true for the Christian. To not be concerned about the consequences of failure would be both unrealistic and a bit foolish. But there is a Christian edge that we need to keep in the forefront of our thinking. We may fail. Our plans may fail. Our organization may fail. But God's work will get done. We need to keep reminding ourselves that the final outcome of God's purposes is never in doubt. The world may judge us as failures, or as Paul put it, "the off-scouring of the world." But God has a different yardstick. He knows the final outcome. He's primarily interested in the love, the fairness, and the justice with which the game is played.

Martin Luther has been quoted as saying, "Sin boldly!" We will make mistakes, but moving ahead in the Lord's name and for His kingdom is worth the risk. God's work will get done.

15

The Tragic Choice

Leaders are constantly involved in choosing. We normally call it decision making. What is actually happening most of the time is selection from a number of possible alternatives. This versus that, or often, this versus those. Indeed, a primary skill of the manager is to make decisions, to make them in a timely manner, and to make a sufficient number of right ones so that the good of the enterprise is maintained.

We all want to make right decisions. There is something in us that would like to believe we are making the right choice. However, too often there is a built-in assumption that we are choosing between "right" and "wrong." This is seldom the case. If we are dealing with strictly technological matters, there may be a right way and a wrong way. But most decisions involve people. And when people are involved, there is seldom a choice that is right for everyone.

Making Right Decisions

John Carnell pointed out that the ultimate problem of choosing is what he called "the tragic moral choice." So often in life we must choose between the lesser of two evils. Carnell illustrated his point with the awful question, "When someone puts a gun to your baby's head, and says he will shoot her if you don't allow him to violate your wife, what do you do?"

The Tragic Moral Choice

Perhaps that seems a bit extreme. Perhaps we are not faced with many moral choices, but consider some of these:
1) A committed Christian brother who has worked for your organization for ten years is causing dissension because of his

Cases

attitude. The morale of the rest of the organization is endangered. You have tried to counsel with him. You know that he is going to have difficulty getting another job. You also know that if you don't separate him from the organization you will be unable to continue your ministry. What do you do?

2) You and your staff are financially stretched to the limit. You have been attempting to carry out a vision you have for the future. You find that you are faced with the choice of using resources you have set aside for the future or watching some of your staff disintegrate under the pressures. It appears to be a question of the people now—or the ministry in the future. What do you do?

3) Your church or organization is involved in a ministry which is attempting to speak prophetically to some of the social sickness you see around you. However, your financial support is coming from a constituency who are really part of the problem. If you speak as clearly as you believe you should, you are going to alienate those who support you. If you don't, you feel that you will violate your conscience. What do you do?

Living Life's Problems

G. N. Tyrell helps us here by understanding life as being made up between "divergent" and "convergent" problems. Most of life is not made up of problems that can be solved technologically (convergent). Rather, "Life is being kept going by divergent problems which have to be lived and are solved only in death." There are few neat answers, but there are some lessons to be learned from organizations which have handled the ongoing problem of choices between wrongs.

When in the Crunch

How can we handle these types of tragic choices?

1) *Recognize that there are probably no easy answers.* If there were, you wouldn't be needed as a leader. The task of the manager is to make choices in the difficult situations.

2) *Gather all the information that time allows.* Often this will not be very much. One of the first questions to ask is, "How long do I have to solve this problem?"

3) *Are there policies, procedures, or rules that cover this problem?* Completely? Partially? What do they say?

4) *Consider the known impact on everyone and everything that is involved.* By "known" we mean what you believe to be true.

5) *Consider the possible impact.* Here we are dealing with speculation. It is often futile to play the "What if . . . ?" game.

70 However, by exploring possible implications of choosing one thing over another, we are sometimes helped from falling into a pit that we might not otherwise recognize. One way to discover

the impact of a choice is to ask if it affects long-range plans or our short-range plans.

6) *Ask if there are ethical and/or moral questions involved.* Sometimes there won't be. Other times they will be disguised. Think about the second and third order impacts as you look for these. If this happens, that will happen, and then what would happen?

7) *Ask if it is possible to reverse the decision once it's made.* Don't fall into the trap of thinking because you made one decision you can't change it. Very often we can decide to change a previous decision.

8) *Ask what advantages there are of having to make a choice.* For example, if you must make a change in the organization, can you use this opportunity to make some other changes that would not have been possible until you made this one? In other words, is it possible to make a feature out of the failure that you seem to face?

9) *Do you really have to choose?* What will happen if you don't make a decision? Perhaps this isn't a problem for you at all.

Finally, to quote St. Augustine again, "Love God and do as you please." God expects us to have courage in making leadership decisions. If we are continually turning over our lives to His control, if we are attempting to live a life of love, and obedience, then we should expect God to honor the decisions we make.

Managing Conflict

How do we manage conflict in a Christian organization? Or should Christian organizations by definition be free of conflict? Does the biblical concept of believers fitting together as a body disallow the presence of conflict?

Conflict within organizations occurs when two or more people disagree on the solution to a problem or the value of a goal. There are different opinions, and different ideas as to what should be done.

How such differences are resolved within an organization says a great deal about the style of leadership that is being exercised. Is conflict permitted in your organization? How is it viewed? How is it resolved? How do you as a leader handle differences of opinion with your peers or subordinates? How do you view criticism (which is actually someone holding a different opinion than yours)?

How we respond to conflict reflects both our view of ourselves and our view of conflict. It will also depend upon our view of power and its use. For if we view conflict as a contest in which one person wins and another loses, the result will be a need to accumulate power so we can win. If we view conflict as an arena in which creativity can flourish and new ideas emerge, then there will be less of a drive toward personal power. But when individuals within an organization sense that conflict is being resolved by the use of power, they will either attempt to accumulate power for themselves or avoid conflict.

There is a close relationship between conflict and creativity.

Strict adherence to the status quo will avoid conflict. It will also eliminate the need for finding new or more appropriate solutions. It is in the struggle for change that the creative juices start to flow. Almost everyone begins life with a high degree of creativity. Through the process of socialization we learn to conform and to suppress our creative urges. A few of us fight this push toward conformity and are usually branded as different, artistic, or even Bohemian. The rest of us must wait for a "safe" environment before we will risk being creative. Conflict then becomes a catalyst to creativity. "Iron sharpens iron."

If we were working with mindless machines or talking about the forces of nature, there would be no need to discuss "conflict." Conflict has to do with people. When an individual or a group sets out to change things, conflict is inevitable. However, it need not be destructive.

Win-Win vs. Win-Lose

Remember the old joke about "Heads, I win—tails, you lose"? In a trite way it reflects a view of interpersonal relationships. Life is seen as a contest in which some win and others lose. The winners get to the "top." The losers never make it.

At the opposite pole from such a win-lose picture of life is win-win. How good it feels to describe a situation in which everybody wins. For most of us such experiences happen all too seldom.

This need not be so. There is a style of leadership which actively promotes situations in which both parties can win. There are ways of managing conflict that view it as not only useful but necessary, and at the same time insist that it need not be destructive.

Win-Win Management Style

What kind of management style permits creative conflict producing feelings that both parties can win?

1) *Begin with clear, high performance goals.* If there is no standard against which to measure the usefulness of a decision, the solutions will tend to be subjective and personal.

2) *Share information up and down the organizational structure.* Bad data produces bad decisions which usually produce bad feelings.

3) *Model appropriate problem-solving approaches.* If the leadership makes unilateral decisions or uses its position to win arguments, the rest of the organization will do the same.

4) *Model a listening ear.* A great deal of emotion is spent in attempting to be heard. If I don't believe you understand my position, how can I accept yours?

5) *Focus on facts, not emotions.* Christian organizations and Christian leaders can unknowingly become very manipulative

by appealing to loyalty, "the Cause," or biblical ideals which may have little bearing on the problem at hand.

6) *Give training in group problem solving.* Many people resort to a bulldozer style of settling differences because it's the easy way or the only way they know. People must learn the skills involved in effective problem solving.

The business of making decisions in an organization is going on all the time. Many are made by individuals without consulting anyone. Often there is no recognition that a decision has been made. But in the midst of all of this there will be discussions, debates, problem-solving sessions in which more than one opinion vies for acceptance. The goal of management is to encourage debate but discourage win-lose situations. How is that done?

Managing Conflict

1) *Insist on facts.* Clearly differentiate between facts and opinion.

2) *View problems as a deviation from a goal.* What is the goal that this problem relates to? The task of the group is to discover solutions that will accomplish the goal rather than enhance an individual.

3) *Break down the problem-solving process* into steps: data-gathering, alternative solutions, trade-offs between solutions, compromise (integration of solutions), and final decision. Too often we force agreement on one solution as a part of a solution before we have adequately explained alternatives. At other times we hold one solution over another, rather than use the best features from both.

4) *Seek to strengthen the power of the group.* The opposite side of that coin is to avoid enhancing the power of one contestant. Keep asking the question, "How can this problem (conflict) be used to everyone's benefit?"

5) *Agree to agree.* The primary tool of the labor arbitrator is to obtain agreement from both parties that agreement is possible and will eventually occur.

6) *Promote effective listening.* We haven't been heard until the other person can accurately state our view. This takes time, patience and a sense that the individual is just as important as the issue at hand.

Conflict, in whatever shape or form it may appear, should be faced and used creatively, and accepted as part of the personal and organizational maturing process. It will always be present and as we face it we must recognize its dangers as well as opportunities.

75

The two Chinese characters making up the word for "crisis" are "danger" and "opportunity." This is what conflict presents to us—both dangers in making judgmental errors and opportunities for moving solidly ahead.

In situations where conflict is faced, pray these through to solutions. Remember that the God who knows the end from the beginning will bring about equitable solutions as we submit our hearts and wills to Him and the leadership of His Holy Spirit.

17

The Anguish of Change

Mrs. Bloomfield had been a member of St. John's Church for twenty-five years. As she walked toward the pastor, who stood waiting at the sanctuary door after the service, it was obvious that she had something on her mind. "Reverend, if Jesus were alive today He would be shocked at the changes in this church!"

There is probably no society in the world which is as accustomed to change as America. We expect change. We assume that tomorrow will somehow be better than yesterday, that new technology will bring "better" things. We expect our children to be smarter than we are. And yet, at the same time, there is the feeling that things have gotten out of hand. Ten years ago Alvin Toffler called it "future shock." Most of us by now are sure that we have had enough of it. Mrs. Bloomfield's nostalgia for the St. John's of her girlhood is typical of the middle-class American longing for "the good old days." More and more Christians, particularly when they think about their local churches, are resisting change.

And with good reason. *All change is perceived as loss.* Even when the change is an apparently happy occasion, like marriage, or moving to a new job, there remains the lingering feeling that something has been left behind, something which we can never recapture.

Christian leaders are change agents. We are in the business of leading people to higher ground, to new adventures, to new accomplishments for God. We have been instructed that change needs to be "managed." But too often as we are managing change, we fail to realize that we are responsible for a lot of anguish.

77

**The
Anguish
of
Change**

We need the change. We need to move to higher ground. We need to mature in Christ. We need to right the wrongs that are out in the world, to change them for the better. But in the midst of our quest, however noble it may be, we not only need a deep appreciation of how to accomplish our goals, but also how to bring about change in a manner that will produce a minimum of distress.

**Why
People
Change**

Change only takes place in people when they are discontent. If we are satisfied with the status quo, why should we change? Skillful union organizers and other mobilizers of public opinion have influenced groups through the discontent of the majority. If one can find enough people who dislike the same thing, then one has a group with a common goal, namely to get rid of that which they dislike. The role of the change agent is then to provide a solution to the common felt need.

But there are also those who are in the business of creating what might be called positive discontent. When the pastor calls us to maturity in Christ on Sunday morning, he or she is creating in us a holy discontent, a discontent with the way we are. We desire to become more than we are. We want to change.

**Resistance
to
Change**

Resistance to change takes place in the same way. If people are presented with new situations that threaten them, the discontentment will be aimed at removing the cause of potential change. The amount of resistance to change will be proportional to the threat to perceive vested interest. It is important to understand that resistance may not be against the change agent or even to the program being proposed. Both may be intellectually perceived as excellent. But however good the program, if it is going to result in what is perceived as changing the way things have always been, it is natural that it will be resisted. Committees or departments can present programs which are obviously beautifully conceived and will in some way produce excellent results for large numbers of people. But time and time again such groups are startled when they present their well thought through plans and are met with cold silence or warm rejection.

The task of the Christian leader is to introduce change in a manner that will challenge and encourage people on the one hand and yet not frighten or discourage them on the other.

78

We noted earlier that Westerners in general, and Americans in particular, tend to focus on individuals rather than on groups. In few societies are the perceived needs of the individual given so much attention. This emphasis on the individual can blind us to how change really takes place. For a number of years sociologists have been describing the change process within groups of individuals as "the diffusion of innovation." They have recognized that when an innovator poses a new idea or does something differently, there will be some who will see the personal advantages to them very early. These "early adopters" are usually in the minority. A second group, usually a majority, will observe how the first is benefiting from the new idea and eventually become "late adopters." Then there is another minority which never adopts the change. The important idea here is that both early and late adopters accept change because they observe its benefits in others. The notion of the diffusion of innovation gives us some insight into how to plan for change, particularly in volunteer organizations, such as local churches.

There are several things a good manager can do to ensure that new changes are accepted. *First, avoid the obvious temptation to make the establishment of the new program, policy, or procedure the end goal.* Too often people feel that once they have gained acceptance—the policy is approved, the procedure is adopted—the task is then completed. Rather, the end goal should allow enough time to demonstrate that the new change is producing good results. We should include some objective indicators to show us if the change is being successful or effective. What are the qualities we might expect to find? For example, if we are going to institute a new worship service in a local church, what would be the indicators that in six months, the worship service is really bringing people closer to God? Or, if we are introducing a new policy on expense accounts, what will be the indicators one year later that this policy is producing the results we want? To give a third example, if we are instituting a training program to train boards, committees, or departments, how will we know that the program was effective one year after the program has begun?

Why such a long time? While the early adopters may be very enthusiastic about the program shortly after its beginning, the majority of the staff or congregation will withhold judgment, or even have negative feelings toward the program, for a longer period of time. In other words, it is helpful to consider how long it will take for everyone to adjust to the situation.

Second, wherever possible, introduce the change to a group smaller than the entire organization. Find a group that is most likely to accept the idea. Indicate to them, as well as to the rest of the organization, that they are really a "pilot study" group participating in a type of experiment. This not only raises the enthusiasm of those involved, but it also relieves the threat to the rest of the group. After all, if it doesn't work with them, then obviously it won't be imposed upon the rest of the group. People are not threatened by change that is taking place in others. And if they are "late adopters," watching what happens with others will often bring them to a point where they are not only ready to accept the new idea, but are actually clamoring for it.

Third, consider the real losses that are going to result as a consequence of the change. Some people are going to lose authority or responsibility. Familiar patterns are likely to be disrupted, as in the case of change in the worship service. In some cases, benefits that accrue to some people are going to be withdrawn. Wherever possible, build into the change plan a way of replacing these losses with some benefit. All change is experienced as loss. But the reason people are willing to accept change is they perceive that the gain, and the feelings associated with it, are greater than the perceived loss.

Fourth, when deciding how to introduce the change leave as much flexibility as possible for how it is to take place. Quite often there are many different ways of achieving the end goal. By inviting discussion on the ways and means of bringing about change, we give people a sense of participation in their own destiny. One way of doing this is to present several (always more than two) ways of achieving the goal, all of which are acceptable. Now, instead of asking people to accept or reject the goal, we are asking them to choose ways of reaching the goal.

Fifth, build in an evaluation system that will identify the early adopters as well as the late adopters. The reason people are late adopters is that they like stability. If you disrupt that stability, they are going to be hurt in some way. If you can identify those hurts, which may not be anticipated ahead of time, you can often modify your plans to help offset the anguish that people will feel. For example, suppose a new policy or procedure has been introduced which changes the relationships between individuals who previously came in contact with one another on a daily basis. You can suggest that these people continue to get together, perhaps once a week, to discuss how the new policy or procedure is affecting them. This gives them the opportunity to express their feelings and to emotionally disengage.

Finally, when introducing change, it is important to look for a win-win situation. Too often, in trying to overcome the objections of other people, we view them as adversaries who have to be won over or even (if only subconsciously) "beaten." We need to remember that the people we are dealing with are brothers and sisters in Christ, and are members of the same body of

Christ of which we are also an integral part. We must try to understand the impact that our actions will have on them and try to prepare them and encourage them. Then the very actions we take will communicate to them that we desire the very best for them.

:|8

Modeling

By modeling we mean a conscious effort on the part of the leader to speak and act in such a way that when the leader is emulated by followers, their actions will be recognized as being appropriate and honoring to Christ.

A Conscious Effort

In what follows, we will not say much about the how-to of modeling. Rather, we will draw attention to the many ways and situations in which we can model.

Nothing seems to impress followers more than the way their leaders respond to situations, particularly emergencies. If our followers see a Spirit-filled calmness in the way we meet unforeseen and difficult crises, they will be inclined to follow our example. If our regular response to others' mistakes is, "How stupid can they be!" we should not be surprised if they respond the same way in front of their subordinates.

Response to Situations

Remaining calm usually means not responding too quickly. If you are one of those people who tend to overrespond to situations, maybe the old adage about counting to ten will help you have enough time to look at the situation objectively.

Leaders usually talk too much. If we dominate conversations or find it necessary to take the lead in solving every problem that a group has, if we are quick to define solutions for other people rather than let them find their own, others will follow our lead.

Listening

We are all impressed by the leader who seems to have the time and ability to hear others out. But it takes practice, as does learning to respond calmly. Everyone wants to believe that they have been heard. If they perceive that their leader has under-

Modeling stood the situation and given their viewpoints careful consideration, then they are more likely to accept it when their leader
chooses a solution different from their own.

Giving Directions The function of leadership is to lead. To lead, one must
understand what needs to be done and how to do it. Leaders
must believe it is in their own best interest and the interest of the
organization to get it done. We can model an attitude which
indicates, "Do it my way!" or, we can model an attitude which
says, "Here is one way to do it which I have found useful. Do
you see a better way?" "Do it my way!" not only prevents others
from jointly owning the goal and having a sense of contribution
to the solution, it also does not teach people how to solve
problems.

Dealing with Subordinates The function of leadership is to lead, not bark orders. There
are prerogatives and perquisites that go with the role of leader-
ship, but if they are carried as though they were the right of the
individual rather than the position, then leadership will be
modeled as a role of personal power rather than a role of
servanthood.

Christians claim that we are part of the "body of Christ." We
claim that within this body each part has a special function.
Indeed, in a way quite opposite to the world's wisdom, we claim
that "those parts that we think aren't worth very much are the
ones that we treat with greater care" and that "God Himself has
put the body together in such a way as to give greater honor to
those parts that need it" (1 Cor. 12:24, TEV).

Integrity If you say something, does your staff believe it will really
happen, or is there always a question of whether you really
mean it? Integrity is not just a matter of keeping our own personal commitments; it involves an understanding that people can
trust us to attempt what we say we will do. Promises should not
be lightly given, unless we want them to be lightly received. An
organization that has a reputation of dealing with its staff in an
equitable and honorable manner must be led by an individual
who personally keeps his or her word to other individuals and to
the group.

Openness Do people see you as someone who is "transparent" and
ready to share your own feelings? Let us not ask others to expose
themselves to a degree that we are not willing to expose our-
84 selves. If you want others to take responsibility for their mistakes, then you need to take responsibility for your own.

Sometimes this means that we need to go out of our way to

point out when a problem really was our fault. At other times in a Christian organization we may need to actually confess our own breech of Christian conduct.

Modeling

The other side of the coin from openness is the need to keep confidences. There is a delicate balance between that which should be shared with everyone and that which should not be disclosed because it was told to you in private. In this dimension we model not only by what we say to our subordinates but what they hear us say to our peers. Also, be careful not to use prayer requests as an opportunity to share confidential information.

Keeping Confidences

Meetings—how much time we spend in them, and how little time we often take to prepare for them! Meetings are inevitable in any organization and exist for a multitude of reasons. Some need to be prepared for with much more care and concern than others. There don't seem to be any courses on how to be a good meeting *participant*. The way people will learn how to participate in a meeting is by following your lead as they watch you participate.

Meetings

What does your office or work area arrangement say about you? Is your office arranged so that visitors must always confront you behind a desk? Are there other chairs or a table to which you can move to make people feel welcome? What does the office layout or the pictures and other decor model for your staff?

Office Arrangement

It almost seems as though some of us were born with a "gift of criticism." It may be the result of extremely high ideals or a lack of self-assurance. But the leader who uses the organization as a scapegoat when things go wrong will usually find that her or his staff shows the same disdain. The leader can manifest this in many ways. The most obvious one is at the time of informing people about their salary: "I'm sorry, but *they* said we don't have enough money." Sometimes it happens when your department, committee or part of the organization fails to get a hoped-for responsibility: "I fought for it, but *they* wouldn't hear of it."

Attitudes about the Organization

We live in a world of "push and shove," a world that is filled each day with another crisis. The "work" can become all consuming. Individual needs can be put aside unthinkingly. We model: "The Work is important, but you (the worker) are not." It is true that in every organization except the local church, the purpose of the organization must come before the needs of the individual. However, this seldom occurs. Most of the time people are more important than the work that we are trying to get

Concern for Others

Modeling done at that particular moment. We need to take the time to affirm others (and let ourselves be affirmed).

We model concern for others in our day-to-day efforts to take time for them and to help with their personal concerns. Modeling can also be demonstrated by the small thoughtful gestures of remembering birthdays and anniversaries, following up on casual prayer requests, appreciating a special effort, and even complimenting a new hairdo!

How Are You Doing? It's not easy to ascertain what we are modeling to our staff. Many times they will not be aware themselves. If they have not had experience in several organizations or with several leaders, they may assume the way we act is the way every organization and every leader acts. How do you discover what they really believe about you as their leader?

One way that has been found effective is to ask each member of the staff to give you an anonymous piece of paper that has a sentence on it which begins with, "I wish Ed would . . ." Then gather the staff together and read out loud the things that they "wished" about you and attempt to address the issues as best as you can. Criticism can at times be startling and very threatening, but by giving your staff an opportunity to comment on your performance you are already beginning to model a willingness to listen, to change, and to become the kind of leader that God wants you to become.

The Wrongness of Being Right

There is something in most of us (Americans anyway) that finds satisfaction in being right about facts and figures. What is more intimidating than the person who, in the middle of a discussion, comes up with something like, "Well, research shows that 38 percent of the people who buy gasoline think it costs too much"? Facts are conversation stoppers. People use them as weapons. The person with a quick mind, or facile tongue seems to "win" a discussion more-often than the one who speaks slowly and thoughtfully.

The trouble is that we tend to take being right very personally. It is as though our being was all wrapped up in what we know. To be wrong becomes a personal issue. It makes us feel bad. It makes us want to win, and to fight back (if that's what it takes to be right).

The result can be a lot of wasted time taken in arguing ("discussing"), and a lot of time spent discovering facts that will serve no other purpose than to prove that we are right. Add to that the tremendous amount of emotional energy that is involved and all the hurts that go along with it, and you will have quite a bill to pay for the privilege of being right.

The kind of thing we are talking about is basically *differences about facts*, which are usually *differences about the past*. Now the past is a funny thing, as anyone who has read a number of history books on the same era can testify. The past is something which exists in the minds of the people who either observed the events of history or heard from those who did. No two people remember it identically. A moment's thought will help us remember the often discussed problem of a number of witnesses who have all seen the same event and yet describe it differently. Why? Why didn't they agree?

First, everyone of us views the world through the lenses of our own presuppositions about the world. We see what we expect to see more often than we see "reality." Two mothers look at a child finger painting on a wall. One sees a creative child, a potential da Vinci. The other sees a messy kid who needs some discipline. You can supply endless illustrations of your own.

Second, everyone acts rationally in their own perception. People do things for reasons that they consider good. What may be an obviously good reason to one person therefore becomes an enigma to another.

Third, Westerners tend to be cause-and-effect oriented. We look for reasons why things happen. So when something happens involving people (as most things do), we start looking for motives. A search for motives very easily leads to placing blame, which in turn soon turns any discussion into an argument.

The Advantage of Not Being Right

In dealing with questions about the past and the circumstances surrounding the past, the chances of our having the correct data are probably no better than 50 percent. Our memories aren't that good. Our biased lens may not have seen the entire picture. Trying to be right about facts that are difficult to prove takes a lot of time, and usually doesn't make any difference in the problem at hand. Why waste precious time digging in a worked-out mine?

Being right can be a losing propostion. If you are right all the time, you will intimidate people, and make it all the harder for them to remember the facts or attempt to share them with you. "No sense in telling old So-and-So. He has his mind made up before you begin." People don't really believe old So-and-So is right all the time. They just believe that this is what he thinks about himself. People in this situation easily become isolated. And the tragic consequence is that they continue to believe that they are right (most of the time), and yet the number of opportunities they have to interact with important events become fewer and fewer.

Another problem with a discussion about someone's attempts to be right is that it easily cuts off the creative juices. Remember the rules of brainstorming sessions: Anything goes. No judgments. No evaluation. Build on one another's ideas. No idea is too big or too small or too far out. In other words, no arguments, no concern about being right, just a concern to contribute to the dialogue.

Wanting to be right can be a big time-waster.

The same thing is true in our personal lives. Parents who need to be right don't listen. Kids who need to be right, which is evidently part of the maturing process, don't listen. It's too bad that so many of us, when we reach 21, are surprised by how much Dad has learned in the last ten years. We don't recognize why he suddenly became so smart.

Husbands and wives have a difficult time reconciling disagreements also. Most men seem to be problem-solvers at heart. Supposedly they are "logical," which is often another way of saying that they can explain the process they went through to reach a conclusion. Many women are supposedly "intuitive," which means that their conclusions may be just as good or better, but they can't explain the process by which they reached them. Many couples find that each partner is trying to convince the other that they are right without listening to the other's evaluation of the problem.

None of us change very quickly. You can teach an old dog new tricks, but it takes longer.

Begin by listening to your discussions. Who does most of the talking? Does it appear that the people you are working and living with are getting a chance to say everything they want to say, or does it look like they get cut off? If it helps, keep an inconspicuous scorepad on how often each person speaks in your next meeting. Are you the one dominating? Or, perhaps you are one of those who lays back and waits for the final say. How many discussions are ended by your pronouncements?

How much time in your next few meetings or one-to-one discussions is taken in establishing facts? How many of these facts were really important? Are you, or is someone you work with, one of those who has to say something about everything?

Listen to the small talk around you. You will discover it's loaded with "facts," most of which are unverifiable, and few of which make any difference.

With this information in hand, see what you can do to change the situation.

Begin by deciding that you have no need to be right. At first that may seem like a big order, and you are sure to find many situations where you feel you must be right. But think a bit. If you are right, doesn't the situation usually turn out that way anyway?

Second, resolve not to argue over things that have nothing to do with the situation at hand. This does not mean to eliminate all small talk. Meetings often need a break to steady it up or get it

Personal Life Too

What to Do about It

Start the Change Process

89

back on the track. Just don't worry about being right about incidentals.

Third, try active listening. Make sure you really understand what someone has said by telling the person what you heard them say.

Fourth, ask the Lord for wisdom. "If any of you lacks wisdom, let him ask God, who gives to all men generously and without reproaching . . ." (James 1:5).

The wisdom the Bible talks about is more than knowledge. It is that innate "sense" which comes as a result of a regular communion with God. It is also the wisdom which comes from knowing His Word and continually walking "in the light" that He gives to us. This wisdom will enable you to contribute meaningfully and significantly to the discussions or conferences you attend.

Finally, focus on the Lord's presence. It's surprising at times how trivial our discussions may sound when we know the Maker of the Universe is listening.

:20

Criticism—Giving and Receiving

Criticism is a loaded word. Although the role of critic is an ancient and respected one, perhaps it is just human nature that has left the word with mostly negative connotations. We will accept this negative usage to the extent that we will discuss criticism as pointing to something which needs to be corrected.

Most people are quick to spot mistakes, but not many give compliments when things are going well, and others are doing what they are supposed to do.

There is a skill or art to giving criticism. There is an even greater skill needed to receive it, particularly from inside our organization.

Criticism has about it a sense of judgment. It is, after all, an evaluation of an individual or situation. For this reason many Christians believe any form of criticism is sub-Christian. We remember the verse, "Judge not, lest you be judged." And yet the Bible continually calls us to a higher standard. When Paul enjoins us to, "Fill your minds with those things that are good and that deserve praise: things that are true, noble, right, pure, lovely and honorable" (Phil. 4:8, TEV), he assumes that we are going to be able to differentiate. Evidently we are going to have to be good critics.

Criticism Is a Two-Way Street

We all have a role. We need to recognize that there are some things outside our right to criticize. When people join our organization, they give us the right to criticize their work and their general performance as a member of the organization, but they do not give us the right to evaluate how they live their

91

Christian lives. The individual will have other relationships outside of the organization, such as family and spouse, which will require his or her own evaluation. Therefore, it is wise to ask, "Do I really have the right to criticize this individual or this situation?" We also need to see that when we invite someone to join our organization, we give them certain rights to criticize us.

What to Criticize

This is a good place to differentiate ends from means. Ends are the goals of our ministry. Means are the ways we achieve those goals. Effective criticism should begin with the goals, and only occasionally be directed toward the means. If the means used to reach the goal are ethical and within organizational policy, we should be slow to criticize just because it wasn't done "our way."

Why Criticize?

Criticism is basically an evaluation. Organizations need to evaluate not only the performance of individuals but also their group performance. Organizations are created for a reason. Someone needs to have the responsibility for evaluating whether the organization and its staff are realizing their purpose.

Too often, many of us are in the habit of criticizing to build our own egos. If I can demonstrate that you are wrong (and therefore I am right), it may help to build my ego. This is a sensitive area because some people seem to confuse a gift for criticism with a gift of exhortation, and therefore, are not aware of what they are doing.

At the same time we need to be careful that we don't surround ourselves with people who will not reprove us. Pastors easily fall into this trap. In a congregation of any size there will always be a few people who value the pastor and his or her actions very highly. These people naturally tend to praise and compliment him or her, while those who may feel negative tend to stay away. We must welcome the suggestions and reproof of others.

We all need criticism. A key way to evaluate our own performance is to measure others' response to what we do. Almost everyone prefers even negative criticism to being ignored.

When to Criticize

Solomon in his wisdom has reminded us that there is a time for all things. Criticism certainly needs to be timely, and administered wisely. The following guidelines should help you when you must confront someone.

1) Personal criticism should never be given in front of others, nor in public.

2) Don't use criticism as a method of rebuttal in an argument.

3) Don't criticize the person. Criticize the action. There's a big difference.

4) Don't criticize in anger. You will usually overreact.

5) Get all the facts. Don't be drawn into a quick response because someone else has given you an emotionally charged account of a situation. There are always at least two sides.

6) On the other hand, criticize as soon as possible after the mistake has been made. Make sure that you know what would have been the correct procedure before criticizing the wrong one. This implies that you have planned times for a critique, times when the performance of the individual or team can be evaluated against planned performance. Planned performance should first be based on what is to be done, second on how to do it.

In an organization, criticism should be given by the individual's immediate supervisor. It is one of the hard tasks of leadership. Don't go around a person's supervisor, and don't let the supervisor avoid his or her responsibility by playing the bad guy for him.

Within the local church, which claims to be the body of Christ, we have a particular responsibility to admonish one another. But this must be exercised with a great deal of caution. In a local church situation it is wise to seek mature counsel before criticizing another. Often you will conclude that criticism will be best received if given by someone other than yourself. Someone distant from the problem or more mature in their Christian life might be a good choice.

Who Should Criticize?

In love.
Clearly
Thoughtfully.
Think about how you word the criticism. Words are like arrows shot into the air. They can often wound someone quite unintentionally. We need to be straightforward, making sure that our criticism is heard and understood. At the same time we need to build up the person. Keep the issues objective, avoiding or postponing emotional involvement whenever possible. Ask yourself how serious the situation is and what caused it. Fit the criticism to the situation.

When criticizing someone, it is helpful to provide an alternative to their wrong action. It is one thing to say, "Not that way!" It is another to say, "Here's a better way." Giving the person an alternative provides him or her with a chance to learn, not just to get a scolding. All of this means that we need to do our homework. We need to understand what is the real problem facing us.

We must also avoid putting negative criticism in writing. First, you may be wrong. Second, the written word has a way of

How to Give Criticism

93

getting around. It hurts to know that other people are privy to your failure.

Receiving Criticism

Nothing is harder to handle than criticism. That is why we must be careful and sensitive as we give it.

Many leaders have particular difficulty in listening to criticism about themselves or their organization, and yet this ability should be a characteristic of every Christian leader. It is hard to accept personal criticism. Often what we do is all wrapped up in what we are. An attack on our actions feels like a direct attack upon our person.

When people criticize us, we need to make sure we are hearing what they are saying. This is a matter of listening. It is difficult for most people to criticize a leader, and often when they finally do it, it is in the midst of an emotional outburst which tends to amplify what is being said. This is why it is best not to immediately respond to such criticism, but attempt to clarify with such sentences as, "What I hear you saying is . . ." If the criticism is justified, the best response is to thank the person and, if necessary, ask their forgiveness.

Seeking Criticism

We need to seek out constructive criticism from responsible people, to really ask for it and look for those who can help us. We can do this through our colleagues, through friends, and sometimes by asking our leader or supervisor. We need to be aware that they may not find it is easy to regularly give constructive criticism.

Don't overlook your spouse. This is a delicate area, and yet your husband or wife is the person who normally knows more about you than any other person in the world.

Self-Criticism

We also need to take the time and make plans to evaluate our own behavior. We should periodically review what we are doing, how we are doing things, and what could be eliminated from our activities. All of this speaks to the need for writing personal goals and scheduling times to evaluate ourselves against our own goals.

Destructive Criticism

From time to time every Christian leader or Christian organization will be faced with criticism which is destructive, either because it is wrong or because of the manner in which it was given. There are a number of alternatives for dealing with destructive criticism. Often the most useful is to acknowledge the fact that you hear it but refuse to respond to it. On a personal level, this may mean a response such as "I'm sorry that you feel that I. . . ."

One of the most effective ways to deal with destructive criticism on a one-to-one basis is to assume that the speaker may have some grain of truth in what he is saying and agree with him:

Leader: "You really did a crummy job of that!"

Response: "I probably could have done that better."

Leader: "You certainly could have. That was terrible."

Response: "It really looks bad."

At this point many people will run out of things to say. Rather than deny what has been unjustly said, it is often better to affirm what is true in the situation without referring to the source of the accusation. Again, timing is important.

Finally, remember that responsible criticism from staff is evidence of a deeper loyalty than tame acquiescence to the status quo.

Listening

We live in an age of increased communication. We are overwhelmed almost every day by the number of messages that are aimed at us: Buy this product. Vote this way. Attend this meeting. Put out the garbage. Be home on time. Get this done. Television, radio, outdoor advertising, direct mail, books, magazines, newspapers, telephone calls, newsletters—all become an overlay on top of our day-to-day personal interactions which also seem to continually multiply. Relationships become shallow, and times of knowing and being known become all too short.

This is the daily milieu in which the Christian leader is called to be effective in giving glory to God. It's not easy.

Too Much Talk

The young and less experienced leader often assumes that the primary task of leadership is to give direction. Perhaps he or she has a picture of a dynamic, hard-hitting manager barking out orders to his or her subordinates. In some situations, such a model may be appropriate, however in most situations it is not only inappropriate but ineffective. We need to learn as early as possible to talk less and listen more. For, as John Drakeford has said in a book of the same title, there is nothing quite like *The Awesome Power of the Listening Ear.*

Why Listen?

Why is it important to listen? The first answer is obvious: When you're listening it's very difficult to talk! "Slow to speak, and quick to listen" has some very practical ramifications. While we are listening we can be thinking. When we are listening we can be attempting to understand what we are hearing.

Listening   When we are listening, we are learning. When we are listening we are giving part of ourselves to another person.

There are probably many jobs that don't require a lot of listening. Not so in Christian work. The Christian leader above any other leader therefore, needs to develop the desire, ability and finally a willingness to help others to listen.

Leadership Earlier we noted that the search for common characteristics
Is of leaders was abandoned years ago. There are none. Leaders
Negotiated come in an infinite variety of styles and philosophies. Current studies on leadership focus on followers, for the one constant attribute of a leader is that he has followers. The question then becomes, how does one get others to follow?

David Secunda, former Executive Vice-President of the American Management Association, who is also an active Christian layman, sums it up this way, "The basic approach to management is to find out what a guy wants and make a deal with him." At first glance, that doesn't seem like a very Christian statement, but let's dig a little deeper. In American parlance a "deal" is a transaction in which both sides are advantaged. To "find out what a guy wants" is to attempt to identify the felt needs of others.

Followers, then, are people who believe that the leader is able to help them meet a need which they identify in themselves. These needs may be as basic as survival needs for food and clothing, or as altruistic as a desire to be more effective as Christian men and women.

The leader too has needs or goals. They will be both personal and organizational. The followers essentially "make a deal" to help the leader achieve these goals.

A major task of the leader is therefore to understand the needs of the followers. This understanding can then be used to determine how the leader and followers can best benefit one another. The leader needs to *listen*.

Steps There are some simple, but often overlooked, steps to listen-
to ing. First, there must be time to listen. There must be suitable
Listening occasions during which the listener is perceived as being available. All the empathy, all the skill in the world are of no value if the person who needs your ear can't get it. Times to listen can be scheduled. But most of the important times come quite unexpectedly. We need to have schedules that are loose enough to permit these important "interruptions."

98   Second, the listener has to be seen as someone who has the ability to understand. This ability to understand is not necessarily a technical ability, but an ability to communicate what

you've heard. As we will see below, often the greatest gift we can give any individual is the feeling that they have been heard.

Third, the speaker must believe he or she has been heard. This belief can come from direct or indirect responses.

If that sounds oversimplified, it isn't. It is hard work.

There are two primary ways of listening—passive and active—and both take considerable skill. **Different Ways of Listening**

The first way to listen is to be available and interested—a smile, a friendly nod, a gesture of concern tells the person that you are with them. This is not as easy as it sounds. Most of us spend the majority of our "listening" time thinking about what we are going to say next, or trying to solve the individual's problem. Because of this we can often divert the conversation completely away from the intention of the original speaker. Most of us are aware that when an individual interrupts us with a problem they often don't get to the real reason for the interruption until the very end. If we start discussing their opening remarks, they may never have enough time to get to the real issue.

It is one thing to hear the words. It is quite another to understand a message. This whole business of "communication" is **Passive Listening** trying to transmit and receive accurate messages. The meaning we assign to a received message often varies greatly from the intent of the sender (speaker). What we "hear" is conditioned by many things: the body language that accompanies the words, the situation or context, the emotion of the receiver, his or her perception about the speaker's intentions, and a host of other things. How often have you assumed that someone was annoyed with you for some hidden reason only to discover later that he or she was evidently unhappy with everybody and everything that day and you just happened to be one of the multitude! Passive listening is the ability to "read between lines" of what one is saying.

This brings us to the second method, usually called active **Active Listening** listening. In active listening we attempt to do only one thing, assure ourselves and our speaker that we understand her. A typical dialogue might go something like this:

"I just don't know how to handle this problem with Joe!"
"He's doing something that really upsets you?"
"Boy, you said it. Yesterday I asked him to pick up the mail before noon, and he arrived at three."
"You were delayed because he was four hours late."

"Not really, but it's his attitude!"

"He doesn't do what you ask."

"Well, usually. But when it comes to the mail, it's always in the afternoon."

"He's let you down on this one thing."

"I don't suppose he lets me down. It's just that he never says no when I ask. He just doesn't do it."

"He seems to have difficulty refusing you."

"That's right. I wonder what I do that scares him."

"He acts like he is afraid of you."

"He really does. You know I'd better see if I can find out why. I really like Joe."

"You think you might find it's something other than the mail."

"You know, it probably is. Well, thanks for listening. It's been good talking to you."

Notice a number of things about this conversation. First, no advice was ever given. All the listener did was attempt to accurately reflect what he thought the other person was saying. He might have immediately started making excuses for Joe or shared his own displeasure with him. In both cases, he would have stopped listening, and the real issue would not have been discovered.

Second, as the speaker listened to herself, through the reflections of another, she was able to gain insight into her problem and take responsibility for it.

Third, because the listener was focusing on the specific content of the speaker, he didn't attempt to solve the problem in advance but rather he let it develop as it went along. The conversation, of course, might have ended in quite another way. But even if the lady who was being bugged by Joe never found a solution for herself, she might at least have felt that she was heard.

Listener's Checklist

Here is a list to help you determine your ability as a listener. Check each one that applies to you.

( ) I usually respond very quickly to the first statement a person makes.

( ) I often lead the conversation off in a direction different from where it began.

( ) When someone tells me of a situation, it usually brings a similar instance that has happened to my mind.

100 ( ) During a meeting I usually do most of the talking.

( ) I usually find out what is going on in my organization indirectly.

If you answered yes to several of these questions, you have some work to do in order to improve your skills as a listener. But be patient, you won t become a good listener overnight.

A good place to start is to work on the planned conversations and meetings you will have. Make a conscious effort to listen. Take notes on what others say if the situation is appropriate. When you are writing, concentrate on what the person is saying and you will find it's difficult to talk.

Work on active listening. Don't be a parrot, but try to re-phrase what you hear (By now "What I hear you saying is . . ." has become a bit overused.)

Keep score on yourself. Be conscious of how you are doing. Notice which of the areas in the checklist require more practice than the others.

22

May I Interrupt a Moment?

How many times have you heard the phrase, "May I interrupt a moment?" in the past few days? Interruptions come in a variety of ways, but most of them are generated by people. There is the out-of-town visitor who "just stopped by to say hello" and is really planning to spend the afternoon with you. There are those phone calls (especially the long distance ones!) which seem so demanding. Most commonly it's one of your peers or subordinates who just needs "a quick piece of information," or who has stopped by to check up on the latest office rumor. Perhaps it is your secretary who passes along that long line of interruptions.

How is the Christian leader to avoid the harassment of continual interruptions?

Begin by taking a look at why interruptions occur, and who causes them.

Why Do Interruptions Happen?

Interrupters are not only your subordinates and your peers, but also your superiors. They need information. The oil of all organizational machinery is information. If it is not applied at the right time in the right place, wheels will begin to squeak, and gears will begin to grind.

For many executives one of the main interrupters is their own secretary. If she is not guilty of trying to get information for herself, many times she has not learned how to protect her boss from the wrong kind of interruptions.

Another reason that people interrupt is that they just want fellowship, or information which will ease the tension of some problem they are facing.

One source of interruptions that many of us seldom identify, is the fact that we interrupt ourselves! Many of us are easily distracted and side tracked. We start doing a task, when suddenly a new thought pops into our mind, or a question arises which needs answering. Before we think, we reach for the telephone, seek out our answer, and then, as we attempt to return to our work, find that we have completely lost our train of thought.

Some people interrupt because they have nothing else to do. Whether they are passing through town, or just passing down the hall, your open door is a welcome invitation to come and pass the time of day.

How to Control Interruptions

We can learn how to control interruptions.

Interruptions from subordinates are the easiest to handle. (After all, you are supposed to be the one in charge!) One way to prevent unnecessary interruptions is to establish standard checkpoints for each task they are given—times when they will report progress to you and discuss obstacles they've encountered. Innumerable interruptions from your subordinates is an indication that they don't know what to do, and that, therefore, not enough time has been spent in planning. Make sure that each of your subordinates is given a written description of the task that he or she is supposed to accomplish and checkpoints along the way. Set up regular meetings with those who need them. If you continue to be interrupted, ask your subordinate why the particular problem cannot wait until your next regular meeting. If it can't, then schedule more checkpoint times.

Open Door?

Should you have an "open door policy?" The open or closed door is an excellent communication device. When you are sincerely trying to avoid interruptions, close the door. When you are ready to receive interruptions, have the door open as a sign that others are welcome. Just make sure that there are times when your door is open. J. B. Phillips' translation of James 1:2 might be appropriate here: "When all kinds of trials and temptations crowd into your lives, my brothers, don't resent them as intruders but welcome them as friends!"

Visitors

Suppose an unexpected visitor does arrive unannounced, either from across the country or from across the hall? What can you do to reduce the impact of such interruptions? As quickly as possible, establish whether the person has a real and immediate need. If your visitor is having a spiritual or emotional crisis, and you're the one who can help, perhaps this is the time to put people before the task. Remember that there is a tension in every Christian organization between getting the work done and caring for people.

Welcome people with a positive indication of how much time you have: "Bill, it's so good to see you! I have ten minutes before my next commitment. What's happening with you. . . ?" Near the end of the stated time, indicate that your allotted time is ending, and ask if there are some other things that need to be discussed before you have to draw the meeting to a close. Stand up as you do this, and remain standing until the final greeting. If it is someone you haven't seen for some time, this would be an appropriate time to pray for each other before you go.

Training Others

Training your secretary and your subordinates, and encouraging the training of your peers and superiors in the art of avoiding interruptions, is a good investment. Discuss with your secretary what words she can use to politely find out how critical is that incoming phone call, and how she can solicit information from the caller that will help her assess whether she should interrupt you. (There are two kinds of people who should always be put directly through: our superiors and members of our family, but make certain your family members don't take advantage of this!) This means that your secretary, as well as your subordinates, need to have a good picture of your schedule. Many executives give their staff a copy of their weekly or monthly schedule and encourage members of their staff to exchange schedules themselves.

Enlist Volunteers

If you are in a volunteer organization, many times you can train part-timers to handle interruptions. Setting up an information center, either a telephone extension or a separate line, which is manned by volunteers, can enable many routine questions to be handled without having to involve the executive.

Environment

Examine the environment in which you are working. Is it conducive to interruptions? Is your desk or office right near the mainstream of office traffic? What about the way your desk is set up within your office? Is it easy for a person to distract you from what you are doing just by standing in the doorway? Rearrange your office situation to cut down on the chance for interruptions, and at the same time to let people know when you're available (such as leaving your door open).

But if changing the office layout won't do it, if the number of telephone and personal interruptions remains high, then maybe the best solution is to put yourself in a different environment.

May I Interrupt a
Moment?   Many executives have discovered that working at home or away from the office one day a week is a very effective way of getting large amounts of creative work done. You don't always have to go home. Perhaps there's another room or office where you can hide. Your secretary can let people know that, "He is not in the office right now, but I expect him back at such-and-such time." (Never put your secretary in a position of not knowing where you are. Someone should always know where you are located, even if you can't be reached.)

Lifestyle   Perhaps the greatest tool you can use to reduce interruptions, is your own lifestyle. As you organize your lifestyle by establishing checkpoints for your subordinates, scheduling your days, leaving "open" time for others, and prayerfully reassessing your goals on a regular basis, and so forth, you will communicate to others the kind of person you are and help them relate to you.

:23

Travel

Travel is one of those "the grass is greener on the other side of the fence" kind of things. People who don't do very much of it wish they did. People who do a great deal of it wish they didn't. Possibly one of the greatest aids to the nineteenth-century missionary returning from the field was the long sea voyage. It usually provided a great deal of time for physical and emotional adjustments to be made.

For the Christian executive today, frequent traveling and moving from one continent to another in less than twenty-four hours can be a trying experience at best. But because time has become such a valuable commodity to those of us in the West, and because we want to be good stewards of that time, it is all too easy to push oneself beyond one's physical, emotional, and sometimes spiritual endurance.

Planning for a Trip

Before taking a trip it's a useful idea to write your own statement of purpose. Why are you taking this trip? What is it you hope to accomplish? What other things might you do while you are there? What will be the consequences when you return? You may discover that the trip really isn't necessary. That will save all kinds of time and money!

In our desire to spread the high cost of travel we often plan too many things into a trip. We need to have a good understanding of our own capabilities and how many hours a day we can afford to spend in each situation. Can you give very good counsel at 11 p.m. after a hard day?

Schedule rest breaks into your day and do your best to see that they don't turn into social events. If people haven't seen you in some time, and/or if you have a reputation for being able to help others, they will tend to overbook you. Often they forget that you are right in the middle of a very busy trip. The only way we know to handle this is to tell people quite frankly that you need the rest and time to be alone with yourself and the Lord.

Think about what you will be doing during the travel time. Perhaps the most relaxing and useful thing you can do is to read a novel or to otherwise "waste time." Others find the privacy of being alone on an airplaine an excellent time to think, pray, or do some of that writing most of us never seem to find time to do. Deciding to do these things ahead of time helps you to move into a trip much more relaxed, and often with a sense of anticipation.

Let people know your intentions. It's very useful to send an agenda ahead to those with whom you're going to meet. You can alert them to the things you'll want to discuss and what it is you hope to accomplish. (This is also a good time to tell them about any rest time you will need.)

Preparation   Adequate preparation for a trip can significantly reduce the amount of potential stress. The following are some helpful guidelines:

1) *Keep a personal travel checklist of all the things you might want to pack for a trip.* Use it as a guide for packing. Many travel agents have these. Get a copy of theirs and then customize it to fit your needs. Remember, there are many places in the world where a small flashlight, your own cake of soap, toilet paper, or even six feet of nylon string to hang your clothes on to dry, are necessities.

Have another checklist of the kinds of working material you might need. You don't want to forget things like notepads, extra pens, a tape recorder, or your address book. Plan ahead.

Leave an itinerary in your office and with your family. It should include the names, addresses and hopefully telephone numbers of where you can be reached in case of emergencies. Leave clear instructions as to under what circumstances you may be contacted.

Take along some standard medicines. This especially applies when you're traveling overseas. Lomotil (a prescription drug) is excellent for handling "Montezuma's revenge." A broad spectrum antibiotic recommended by your doctor is also useful, as are such things as cold remedies and aspirin. And don't forget to get any innoculations you might need well in advance. Three shots in one arm in one day can be terribly painful.

Wherever possible plan to travel light. Most airlines will allow you to carry on a garment bag with pockets in it as well as an under-the-seat briefcase. It is wise to carry some toilet articles and a light change of clothing with you.

We are all familiar with *the problems of jet lag*. Most of us can handle the three-hour time change we have flying across the United States, but beyond that jet lag can be a real problem. We also need to understand that some of us don't sleep well on airplanes. Usually you won't need a rest the moment you arrive, but within 12 to 24 hours you will need a time for catching up. Plan for it, and put it into your schedule.

2) *Watch your eating.* It's much better to skip a meal than to overeat. Our biochemistry needs to get restabilized, both for the time change and the difference in food.

3) *Try not to begin a trip already tired.* If you see that you're going to have a very heavy schedule before you leave, consider leaving a day early, or spending a day alone with your wife, husband, or family at some place away from home.

4) *Plan reentry time.* This can be done in the middle of a trip or at the end. We all need reentry time with ourselves, with our families, as well as our work. Sometimes you can combine all three of these by planning a short working holiday with your wife or husband. Three days during which you spend a half of each day catching up with business correspondence (brought along by your spouse!), and the other half day catching up with your family. You will then be able to return to the office prepared for the situations there and prepared for the needs you'll encounter within your family.

If you have children, while you're away your husband or wife has to act as both mother and father. Over a period of weeks family members will readjust themselves to this situation. But it can be a very jolting experience, for example, to have a father come home from a trip and start making decisions for the family again! Discuss this with your family both before and after the trip. It makes reentry a lot easier.

Develop a standard list of questions that you need to ask concerning your ministry wherever you go. In addition, have a list of questions that you plan to get answered at every place you're going to visit. One very helpful tool is to organize your trip by setting aside a manila folder for each place that you're going to visit. As you correspond back and forth with people prior to your trip, you can put relevant information in each correspondence folder. When you're ready to go, pull out the folders and take them along.

Next, get your address book up-to-date. Some people find it appropriate to break their address books down by continent or

Travel   country or state so that they're sure to touch base with the proper people when they're in each place. Remember that even though you can't visit with a lot of people, just making a telephone call to them can be very appreciated. Some people find it useful to jot down the names of family members, secretaries, and others, along with the name and address of the people with whom you'll be in contact. (A loose-leaf address book makes this task easier.)

If the trip is going to be of any extended duration, then you need to think about the appropriateness of a phone call home at a predetermined time. Travel can be disruptive to families as well as individuals. Your family is important!

Briefing   If you are visiting people or places you've never encountered
Yourself   before, it's an excellent idea to get a briefing on both. There is plenty of information available in the local library. Try to get some understanding of the religious, political, geographical and cultural situations into which you're going to go. (By the way, if you're planning to use credit cards make sure the countries you're going to will honor them.)

Mind   How you think about a trip before you take it is very impor-
Set   tant. If you think of it as being burdensome and a chore, it will usually be difficult. If, on the other hand, you think of it as being a special time which can be used receptively and profitably it can easily become a joy.

Those of us who have the opportunity to travel need to see it as a privilege.

110

24

Need a New Secretary?

There are few things more important to the effective, successful executive than a good secretary. The Christian leader who has the privilege of having a secretary and yet does not use her to full advantage, is missing a real opportunity for personal growth and improved leadership.

We refer to a secretary as "her." This is not only a recognition of the current situation, but also reflects a belief that, at least in our Western culture, women have some basic qualities that seem to fit with the needs of a leader for an executive secretary.

Basic Qualities

The particular way in which an executive and the secretary work together, will be dependent on the executive's style of doing his or her job. But there are some basic qualities that every executive should look for in a secretary:

1) *Loyalty.* Without it, you are defeated before you begin. It starts, of course, with the common and highest loyalty to God, for our Christian service is given to Him. But there needs to be a complete loyalty to you. This need not come at the expense of loyalty to others or to the organization. But it does imply a confidential relationship and trust. Your secretary sees you as you are.

2) *Memory.* Not many secretarial books talk about it, but a good memory, and especially what we would call a "connective memory," can do much to help your performance. The best of filing systems will fail. Calendars will be overlooked. Your desk may become a shambles. The secretary who can find "it" soon becomes invaluable (sometimes *too* invaluable!).

111

3) *Maturity*. It takes maturity to maintain a pleasant smile in the face of an irate visitor, to know that the best of bosses will have a grouchy day, and to carry a warm, friendly, cheerful spirit, without being effusive or aggressive.

4) *Insight*. She needs to be able to learn how you think, to study your work habits, to become almost "alter ego." Her greatest value as an executive secretary is to be able to make decisions the way you would make them yourself.

5) *Self-Organization*. Let's face it. Most executives are so busy organizing other people and things that we need someone to organize us. To do that, a secretary needs to be organized herself. This means planning her day in a way that permits interruptions. It means not being thrown by unexpected events. It means knowing where everything is and how to use the tools available.

6) *Alert to details*. Executives need to have the "big picture" continually before them. As a leader, you may have a day filled with far-reaching decisions. Someone other than yourself better pay attention to the details, and that someone is usually your secretary. A good secretary will notice the details and see that they are handled or gently remind you that you need to handle them before they become big problems.

7) *A model and a trainer*. Being an executive's secretary, gives many secretaries the opportunity to train other staff. They can do this by what they do and by what they say.

8) *Attractive*. A good secretary takes care to see that she is dressed neatly and appropriately, and is well groomed. But an attractiveness of attitude and spirit is the most important component of true beauty.

9) *Skills*. Typing and shorthand skills are necessary but many others are also important. She needs interpersonal skills in handling people, an understanding of basic office procedures from simple accounting to how to get her typewriter repaired, not to mention travel planning and schedule juggling.

How to Find Such an Angel

Now if your secretary has all of these qualities already, blessed are you among executives. Suppose she does not. What can you do about it?

Take your time in hiring a secretary. Look for a balance between enthusiasm and experience and education. Check references by phone if you can. Look for a fit in your personalities and outlook.

You are going to spend hundreds of hours with this person! Pay the extra expense of temporary help while waiting to get the right person.

Once you have hired a secretary, there are several things you should do.

1) *Take time to train her.* Put training time down on your calendar. A good secretary will eventually figure out what you are up to, and be grateful for your time. Expose her to all the people she will need to know. Personally introduce her to your peers and superiors. Lead her through any organizational procedures that may exist. Tell her your idiosyncrasies, your likes and dislikes. Take time to tell her *why* as well as *what.*

2) *Maintain communications.* Set aside a few minutes at the beginning of each day to review both of your workloads with her. Let her help you figure out how you are going to get your job done and then help her with hers.

3) *Delegate clearly.* There are many levels of delegation. Make sure she knows what decisions you want her to make and which are to come back to you. Do you want her to compose replies to letters before showing them to you? Which ones? What kinds? Do you want her to maintain control over appointments, visitors and phone calls? Under what circumstances? How?

This is a very delicate area. Your secretary is "you" to many people. It is very difficult for others to question whether she is "interpreting" what you are saying, or actually giving a straight story. Encourage your secretary to develop mutual trust with others so that they feel free to come to her, and yet at the same time they do not expect to get special favors.

4) *Plan together.* Your job is her job. The more she understands what you are up to, the more responsibility she can assume. Planning can take many forms. One of the best ways is to make sure that you have a calendar which reflects what you are doing. There's nothing more embarrassing for a secretary than not to know what her boss's plans are. This may involve a lot of calendar juggling, but in the long run it will pay off.

5) *Let her initiate.* Let her sort out the mail into categories such as "Immediate Attention," "Look at Today," and "Reading." Have her read your mail and note things to be handled, replies needed, items someone else can handle. Encourage her to dream up Plan B when Plan A fails; teach her how to do it.

6) *Give her ongoing training opportunities.* Encourage her to attend training seminars, to join secretaries' societies, to take college level extension courses.

7) *Pay her for the level at which she is working.* If she is doing the job of an *executive* secretary, make certain that within the confines of your organization's salary structure she is paid as an executive secretary. (She may be worth more than some executives!)

113

8) *Set high standards.* Excellence is hard to attain, but it is worth the effort. If there is time to do a job over, there was probably time to do it right in the first place.

9) *Increase her responsibility.* Keep expanding her role as far and as fast as she can go. Plan on making her the best secretary you have known.

10) *Appreciate her.* It's so easy to get caught in the daily office routines that we fail to notice growth and improved performance or even little jobs well done. How easy it is to be appreciative of everyone else and fail to give a well deserved compliment to the one working closest with us.

11) *Maintain a professional relationship.* The more effectively your secretary does her job, the more personal will become your relationship. This is an advantage. It can also be your greatest point of vulnerability. How many men do you personally know who have destroyed their careers as the result of an improper relationship with their secretary? The reasons are obvious. Daily contact, a deep understanding of your needs, a constant attention to your desires, all contribute to building a very attractive relationship. If this is combined with less than adequate support at home, the results can be disastrous. There's no easy answer to this problem except to recognize the potential for trouble and to insist that you both act accordingly. Avoid situations that could be in any way compromising. It may cause inconvenience, but it will be worth it in the end.

12) *Plan for her replacement.* Soon after she comes to work for you have her start compiling a notebook on how you want things and how she does them. Most secretaries put off this kind of work since (at the moment) they have no intention of leaving. But to have a well-tabbed notebook on such things as letter format, handling phone calls, logging and filing letters, arranging trips, and handling expense sheets can save many, many hours of frustration when she leaves.

25

On Getting Overcommitted

One of the costs of leadership is a loss of personal freedom. This is a paradox. On the face of it, it appears the more one's authority and breadth of responsibility increase, the more control there should be over one's own time and commitments. But increased responsibility goes hand-in-hand with more focused commitments. The head of an organization of any size quickly discovers that the great majority of his or her time must be closely related to that organization.

Higher Visibility: More Demands

The world is attracted to successful people. Christians are not very different. The effective Christian leader discovers that as personal advancement occurs, so do opportunities for "public ministry." Requests come to speak at this meeting or that conference. Other organizations seek counsel and advice. Invitations are extended to serve on boards and committees. Your presence is "needed" at an ever growing number of important meetings. The calendar fills up months in advance and sometimes years in advance. What seemed like an innocent commitment to speak or write or attend a meeting, eighteen months ago, suddenly is absorbing large chunks of unexpected time. Personal and ethical dilemmas abound. "Should I keep that commitment, or should I spend that long promised vacation with the family?"

If this is the kind of situation in which you find yourself, there are some positive steps you can take to get your life more ordered. If you sense that you are moving into this kind of a situation, there are also things you can do to avoid it.

*On Getting
Overcommitted*

**Taking
Stock**

**What
Is
the
Purpose?**

**How
Much
Time
Will
It
Take?**

**What
Priority
Does
It
Have?**

**What
Should
You
Do
About
It?**

**Do You Really
Have the Time?**

116

We need to ask the same question of all of our time commitments that we would ask of any major commitment of our life. After all, "life" is made up of all the pieces of our "time."

Take out your calendar and review it. For each of the items in your appointment book answer each of the following questions.

1) *What is the purpose?* Why are you doing this? Is it part of your basic task in your organization? Is it contributing to your family? Does it have something to do with your particular calling and role in God's kingdom? Who will benefit by it?

2) *How much time will it take?* How long will it take to prepare for this particular appointment? What do you have to do to get ready for it? If it is outside of your home or your office, how much time will it take to get there? How much time will it take to plan what needs to be done? How many meetings or other activities will have to take place as a result of this one?

Think of all the different ways that your commitment to this particular appointment can involve you in time. Add them all up and note the total number of minutes, hours or days.

3) *What priority does it have?* When you think about priorities, think about your personal and spiritual commitments, your commitment to your family, and your commitment to your local fellowship. When you think about all of your other commitments, what priority do you give this one?

4) *What shall I do about it?* There are a number of possibilities. You could go ahead just as you planned. You could find ways of doing it more efficiently or more effectively. Perhaps you could combine this task or commitment with another one. Perhaps you could postpone doing it. Maybe it's something that doesn't have to be done when you have it down in your appointment book.

What would happen if you abandoned it completely? Who would be hurt? What goal would not be reached? Would there be adverse consequences for someone else that might offset the positive consequences for you?

5) *Do I really have the time?* Usually our appointment books and calendars show the time of the events themselves. Sometimes we note the travel time that might be needed to get to a place. But seldom does one find on an appointment book something like "9:00–12:00—prepare for meeting with group leaders." For each of the appointments and events to which you are

committed, block out the time it will take to prepare for that particular situation. In other words, where necessary, make a date with yourself to do what has to be done.

6) *What have I forgotten?* Sadly, our appointment books tend to be filled up with tasks and business commitments. Does your appointment book show some time blocked out for your family? Do you have some dates with your husband or wife or your best friends? Have you blocked out some time to be alone with God's Word and let the Spirit speak to you? What would your appointment book look like if you put down these times?

What Have You Forgotten?

Have you thought about putting down times when you are going to schedule nothing, times when others can reach you with their problems?

As you begin to think about your present commitments in light of how much time they are likely to consume, you may discover that some of the things which seemed like a high priority when you first went through the list, now seem much less important. Begin by reviewing the commitments which are furthest into the future and consider the possibility of withdrawing now. This will create the least amount of havoc among those to whom the commitment was made.

Time to Cancel?

Continue to move back closer to the present. Do you really have to keep that commitment? Can you think of something that would have a higher priority that would cause you to automatically give this one up? A good exercise is to ask yourself what would happen if you broke your arm. Would the world go on without you?

Stay flexible. We have to keep telling ourselves this over and over. Leaders tend to have a high level of commitment. They tend to be busy people who take on a large number of tasks. Many demonstrate the old proverb, "If you have a big job to do, find a busy person to do it." But there is another more modern proverb to remember, "You can never get an hour's work done in an hour." Don't get uptight when things don't go 100% according to plan.

Stay Flexible

For the Christian there is a close relationship between planning and prayer. If it has not become a part of your natural process, you may want to add one more question to your list: "Is this a commitment I believe God wants me to keep?"

Go in the Spirit

117

:26

The Executive and the Family

It is our profound conviction that there are three levels of priority for the Christian, and the relationship between these priorities is of prime importance. These priorities relate to the whole structure of our relationships, including our relationship to our family.

Three Levels of Priority

Our first priority is obviously God through Christ. The Bible leaves no room for disagreement here. Our commitment to God must be ultimate (Matt. 22:36–37).

The second level of priority is not so universally appreciated. The Bible calls us first to a commitment to God, but second to a commitment to one another. The biblical concept is that the work of Christ is carried out by His church, not by individuals (Eph. 4:12f.). Indeed, the New Testament focuses primarily upon the relationship of believers to one another and to the world, rather than to the work they are to carry out.

A third level of commitment is to the work of Christ. And yet it is clear from Ephesians 4 that this work is to flow forth from a unique combination of gifts given to individuals for the building up of the body of Christ.

What effect does success have on a person? As an individual rises to a place of leadership in an organization and becomes conscious of making significant contributions to the growth and welfare of the organization, the work can become more and more exciting. Past successes generate enthusiasm for new ventures. We can easily become stretched beyond our own capabilities. Fatigue, and its accompanying sense of despair, can

The Other Side of Success

119

drive us on to new endeavors, rather than warn us to slow down. Beware.

Success can also produce tension between a husband and wife. Are both partners going in the same direction? Is the wife or husband of the Christian executive called to the same work? Traditionally, when a pastor has been called to a church, the congregation has assumed the wife was part of the package. The wife was seen as an extension of her husband. This view is more and more being rejected by younger wives. On the other hand, organizational wives are often viewed as a source of discontentment and potential gossip. How is your partner viewed? Where does he or she fit into your success?

The Second Priority

If you are one of those men or women whose life is completely centered around the work to which God has called you, then we would suggest the need for an ongoing reevaluation of your commitment to the body of Christ, and particularly to your family. Use those same skills which have brought you success in your organization, to evaluate the health of your family. Here are a number of areas that you may want to look at:

1) *Your appointment book.* Most of us put down in our appointment books those engagements which have the highest priority in our lives. Are your spouse and your children down in your appointment book? If your wife and your children analyzed the way you are spending your time on the basis of your appointment book, would they feel that they have a significant priority in your life? Have you taken your teenage son or daughter out to lunch recently? Perhaps your schedule is full this month, so plan ahead!

2) *Your understanding of your call.* Have you shared this with your family? They need to understand what it is you do and why you do it. It is amazing how many children have misconceptions of their parents' work. Have you let your children spend the day with you at work? Have you ever walked them through your organization's facilities and explained to them how things work? What about taking your children on a business trip? If you are a person who is required to do a considerable amount of traveling, what about saving ahead so that your wife can accompany you on some of these trips? She can see what you do first hand, meet some of the people you go to see, and experience some of the travel stresses you have.

3) *Times with the family.* Too many executives take their work into their homes with the result that the "work" is quickly viewed by the children as competition with them. Many executives and pastors encourage people to contact them at home,

with the result that the family can develop a "them and us" mentality. This is a particular problem for the pastor. Careful attention must be given to protect times with the family.

Once this time is secured, it needs to be quality time. It is all too easy to be in each other's presence without really experiencing each other's person. This may require considerable advance planning for such things as an evening of games, a day away at a park or beach, or some other mutually enjoyable experience. Take a look at your children's calendars. Are there going to be special times like ballgames in which they are participating or other events that they would like you to attend? Older children in school or away from home, still need you too, even though at times they may not seem like it.

4) *Family devotional time.* This is an area that can quickly be neglected by the Christian leader with "greater" responsibilities. It becomes especially difficult when times of family worship and prayer are viewed as something "we have to do because of Dad's work." Visit your local Christian bookstore for help here. Don't assume that because you're an effective pastor or because you're a well-known speaker you have insight into what would be appropriate for children and families. Many good books are available to give you creative ways to make these times fun and worthwhile.

5) *Vacation times.* We suggested earlier that you use some executive skills to strengthen the health of your family. In the type of merry-go-round world in which we live, our only defense against the unbearable number of demands placed upon us, is to start planning into our lives those things which we believe would be honoring God and healthful to ourselves and to our families. Compare your calendar with your spouse's and children's. What do they tell you about the way you're spending your time? When can you set aside extended time to be alone with you family and build into each other's lives?

A Christian executive shared with us his frustrations of being **One** so involved with his work that his family always suffered. No **Man's** matter how hard he tried, he arrived home each evening still **Experience** full of the day's problems. He tried the suggestion of leaving his worries on a "Worry Tree" in the front yard. It didn't work.

Finally, he sensed the Lord was telling him he was going about it in the wrong way. Rather than empty his mind of his concerns, he saw that he should fill it with thoughts of his family. His drive home was about five miles. He picked out conspicuous landmarks along the way and associated them with specific members of his family. As he passed each one he tried to imagine what that family member would have been doing that day, what special concerns he would have, or what she would like to discuss with him that evening.

By the time he walked up the front path his mind was full of his family. Now the cries of "Dad's home" began to take on new significance. As he expressed it, Dad was *really* home, and the family knew it.

**We
Are
Made
for
Relationships**

The most important part of God's creation is people. Relationships are what life is all about. No matter how high our spiritual calling, the basis of our effectiveness is our effectiveness as members of the mystical body called the Church, and the love we have for one another. If you are looking for a measure of your effectiveness, check out the love life within your family.

:27

When Did You Leave Your Wife?

Here's a little test for you to take:

( ) I usually take work home at night.
( ) I haven't had a date with my wife in two weeks.
( ) I don't have a date with my wife listed in my appointment book.
( ) I usually work away from home more than 10 hours a day.
( ) We have had two fights in the last two weeks.
( ) We haven't had a fight in five years.
( ) I have at least four more years of education than my wife.
( ) We married before I was called to my present task.
( ) Our youngest child is between 16 and 20.
( ) My wife hasn't been on a trip with me in four years.
( ) Most of our social relationships are related to my work.
( ) We've been married 15 to 20 years.
( ) The family dinner is often interrupted by phone calls for me.
( ) My wife has little understanding of how my organization works.
( ) My wife does not have any career plans outside of our marriage.

If you marked very many of these statements, you may have already left your wife.

We are addressing ourselves here as Christian leaders, and especially as married men. Where does your wife fit into these priorities? Certainly of all the interpersonal relationships described in the Bible, the highest and most mystical is the relationship found in marriage. Paul could only compare it to the relationship of Christ and His church (Eph. 5:21–33). The disruption of this relationship can have tremendous spiritual consequences. Peter tells us that problems in the relationship can even interfere with our prayers (1 Pet. 3:7).

Is your ministry as a Christian leader built upon a foundation of a strong marital relationship, or does it move forward in spite of that relationship?

**Where
Is
Your
Wife?**

**What
About
Your
Calling?**

Some of us immediately respond in our own defense, "But this is the ministry to which God has called me! My wife understands that. That's one of the sacrifices that we are making together." Perhaps. But perhaps that is your view of the situation, and although it may be outwardly shared by your wife, perhaps inwardly she feels quite differently.

Too often the Christian wife is put in the position of appearing to oppose the will of the Lord if she does not feel at ease with the circumstances within which her husband is functioning. Many men and women marry before they have a clear picture of the ministry to which they (or he) may be called. Too often they overlook what the Spirit may be saying to *her* and what gifts God may have bestowed upon her.

**It's
an
Uphill
Battle**

The wife of a dynamic pastor or Christian leader is in an uphill battle for survival as a person. Many times she has sacrificed herself and her own education only to see her husband be educated right out of her intellectual sphere. The public affirmation that comes to him, the sense of accomplishment he feels in pursuing his career, can only be shared by her in a secondhand way.

Of course, there are many husband/wife teams who really are teams. They truly have a common call to the work for which the husband is employed. They see themselves as sharing a joint ministry. But for most this is far from the case. And as the initial intensive occupation of raising a family and "becoming established" is exchanged for the changing realities of mid-life, many wives of executives (Christian and otherwise) begin to wonder whether this is all there is to living. Many conclude that it is not.

**What Can You
Do About It?**

What can be done? Begin by taking the statements at the beginning of the chapter and asking yourself, "What does this mean?" to each of them. The answers to this question may suggest to you some steps which you could take immediately.

124

1) *Start asking your wife for dates.* Make these times for just the two of you. Use them to explore how she feels about what she's doing and what you're doing. For example, share your

appointment books and calendars together. What do you jointly think about the way you're spending your time? Who have you been with? Who are your friends?

2) *Ask her to evaluate how she sees you spending your time.* What does she picture you doing? For each item does she feel you spend too much time, or too little? Does she think you are doing fine? Does she have suggestions from which you could benefit?

3) *Make a list of your individual and joint commitments.* List commitments to things like work, children, friends, the bank, church, whatever. To how many things are you committed together—independently?

4) *Dream about the future together.* Try to fantasize what you believe would be the very best situation for you as individuals and as a couple ten years from now. Where would you want to be living, what would you be doing, what would your relationships be? What are your wife's gifts? What is her calling? Where do her gifts and calling fit into the picture for the future? Together set some long-range goals for you as individuals, and for you as a couple. Decide on some immediate steps to meet those goals.

5) *Consciously reschedule your life.* Leave blocks of free time to do spontaneous things together. Consciously leave some time unscheduled so you can be free to better respond to each other's needs. We can't instantly change our lifestyles, but we can begin to take concrete steps to keep from letting our desire for success interfere with our families.

6) *Evaluate the three levels of priorities.* Prayerfully consider whether you really do believe that the priorities suggested above are biblical and operative in your life. God's work will get done without you! God is really not nervous about the future. Isn't He much more concerned with what you are than what you accomplish? And isn't what you are demonstrated by the relationships you have? And isn't the most profound of those relationships the one that you have with your wife?

Have you left your wife?

We pray she will take you back.

:28

Stress

"If she says that to me one more time, I think I'll scream."

"If we get another bill like this, I don't know what I'm going to do."

"You better not go near Jim today. He's really uptight."

"What a lousy night. I stayed awake half the time worrying about whether Jan and Pete are really going to make it."

What is the common denominator in all of these? Stress. What is stress? Actually, it is the spice of life. In all types of activities we are involved with stress. When we exercise our muscles we are stressing them. When we exercise our minds we are stressing them. Life without stress would be dull indeed. But the problem most of us face, far too often, is too much stress and strain. It seems so hard to cope.

The difficulty is that we have little understanding as to why some things cause more stress than others, or why certain kinds of stress in one person's life cause an entirely different kind of reaction than they do in another. By now almost all of us are aware of the fact that there is an intimate relationship between physical, emotional and spiritual stress.

Your Uniqueness

Everyone in the world is unique. There never has been another you, nor will there ever be one. Even twins don't have identical fingerprints. It follows that each one of us tolerates the stresses in our life differently. Our need is to know ourselves well enough that we can apply our gifts and skills in ways which will strengthen us through stress rather than weaken us through distress. The apostle Paul puts this in the right context. In the twelfth chapter of Romans he comments, "Don't think of yourself more highly than you should. Instead, be modest in your thinking and judge yourself according to the amount of faith that God has given you" (Rom. 12:3, TEV). This is not to put us down. Rather it is to be accepting of who we are. Does it not follow that Christians, of all people, should be able to accept themselves, should see that their gifts and experiences are given to them as stewards of God's good grace?

Accept Yourself

A lot of our stress is the result of never being satisfied with ourselves. Accepting oneself is not easy to do, particularly in a Western society which is continually calling us to become something other than what we are. We should be more handsome, more beautiful, be the owner of a prestigious automobile or a larger home. The whole point of advertising is to make us dissatisfied with ourselves.

No one is perfect. No one does everything well. But everybody does something well. Knowing what your gifts are can be your best asset.

Accept yourself at the age you are. Anticipate the good things that are yet yours, rather than regret what might have been. God is not playing games with us. He is the One who is *for* us! Accept your position in life, not in the sense that you cannot move forward, but rather in the sense that at this moment you are what you are, and God is able to use you where you are. He created you. You are loved by Him . . . and He likes you too!

A Few Hints

1) *Don't overschedule your day.* You can rarely do an hour's work in an hour. There will be interruptions so plan for them. Leave time at the end of each period to take a breather. Relax, waste a few minutes. You'll enjoy it. And, it will be good for you.

2) *Know what you're going to do in the next twenty-four hours.* Start the day with a list of things you want to accomplish. Start with the ones that are top priority and emphasize working on those.

3) *Fit the amount of time needed for a job to the job.* Too often we try to do a large job in bits and pieces. At the other extreme we are prone to push too long on some things, like preparing a report or a sermon. Stress becomes distress when we have too much of the same thing or spend too much time on something. That's why stress in one area, such as exercise, can relieve distress in another area.

4) *Plan to reward yourself with some breaks in the routine.* A relaxing game of golf, a few hours reading a new book, or a day off with your children, can do much to calm and refresh you.

5) *Face new situations realistically.* Ask yourself if what con-

fronts you is really worth fighting for. Will changing this person's opinion or correcting that situation really make a
difference ten years from now?

6) *Strive for excellence in a few things.* Understand the limits
of your abilities and with those abilities do the best you can.
Don't strive for perfection. That is almost always unobtainable.
It is the perfectionists who are the most frustrated of all people.

7) *Recognize the interrelationship between stress and physical
well-being.* Frustrations, insecurity, and general unhappiness
are directly related to such things as ulcers, hypertension, and
backaches. Loosen up. It'll do you good!

8) *Have at it.* When you have to tackle something that is
really painful and it is something that you have to do, don't
hesitate. Get it done now. Put it behind you. The final accomplishment brings a great feeling of satisfaction.

9) *Be yourself.* God created you and you are unique in His
sight. He cares for you and has identified Himself with you.
Relax and be the person you were meant to be.

"Don't be worried on account of the wicked; don't be jealous
of those who do wrong. They will soon disappear like grass that
dries up; they will die like plants that wither. Trust in the Lord
and do good; live in the land and be safe. Seek your happiness in
the Lord. And he will give you the desires of your heart. . . . Be
patient and wait for the Lord to act; don't be worried about those
who prosper or those who succeed in their evil plans. Don't give
in to worry or anger; it only leads to trouble" (Ps. 37:1–4, 7–8,
TEV).

:29

Do You Have an Education?

Notice that we didn't ask have you had an education, but rather, do you have one? Education is the process that we all go through in order to cope with the world in which we live. It enables us to accomplish those things in life that we believe we are led to do.

The Christian has a special advantage here. He or she believes that God is at work in him to continually make him more than he or she is. (It is God who works—keeps on working—in us, both to will and to do His good pleasure. [Phil. 2:13].) We are people in process.

We are all familiar with the tremendous advances in the area **Changing** of technology. What is not so obvious is that the number and **Roles** types of roles we play are also being affected by technological changes. Consider the variety of roles expected of the local church pastor. He or she is supposed to be preacher, manager, executor, leader, counselor, exhorter, teacher, planner, laborer, and it goes on.

If you are not personally involved in a program of continuing education at this moment, now is the time to take action. The longer you wait the more difficult it will be. None of us would ever consider that our Christian education is complete. Don't get trapped into believing the rest of education is ever complete.

Education for most Christian executives, is primarily concentrated in the knowledge area. We call this "education for the task." As we move ahead in our God-given profession, we need to learn more and more about how an effective organization

131

**Education
for
What**

works and all of the factors that are associated with it. We also need to learn interpersonal skills as well as a growing number of basic skills on how to cope with the technological changes in our society.

What do we mean by *education for "the system"*? Organizations of any size tend to be complex. They not only have their internal complexity, but the complexity of their relationships to the other organizations with whom they relate. For example, a foreign mission society has home office personnel, home country area personnel, overseas personnel and an overseas church. All these relationships fit together to make up the "system" which is the organization. To survive, this organization must continually adapt itself to changing circumstances. This means new rules, new regulations, new policies, new ways of doing things. We call this "education for the system."

We don't often think about education for society. But each of us somehow fits into the society in which we live. We have responsibilities toward our society, and the society in turn interacts with us. We must learn what our responsibilities are, and remember that they are not static. Any missionary who has spent four years in another country and then returns to his home country has experienced "reverse cross-cultural shock." What a difficult process this fitting-in can be!

**What
Are
the
Means
of
Continuing
Education?**

Once one decides what the educational need is, the next step is to select from various means available for training and continuing education. There may be a compromise between what is optimum and what you can afford. Some helpful sources for education are:

1) *Professional journals.* Journals and publications are basic to any professional, whether secular or Christian.

2) *Books.* Those in your field are a must. Some organizations keep a small organizational library which they rotate among their staff. Supplement this with a book allowance. Anything that can be done to encourage reading on the part of the staff is to be commended.

3) *Miscellaneous sources of information.* Helpful information selected by various staff members can be passed around within the organization for the benefit of others.

4) *Professional seminars.* Seminars are available which deal with a multitude of topics. They can last from one hour to three weeks or longer. Many of these are offered in conjunction with university programs. Get in touch with the continuing education program of your nearby university or ask to be put on the mailing list of universities that you know offer such programs.

5) *Sabbatical leave.* Perhaps you need to consider the need for an extended leave for the purpose of study.

6) *After-hours formal education.* In many cases the organization will finance such education. The availability of nearby colleges and universities will of course be a consideration.

7) *In-house training programs.* These can be used to teach more specific skills as well as philosophical concepts. There are many sources available on almost any subject. See the Yellow Pages.

Do You Have an Education?

If you have been away from any formal training program for ten years or more, you may think that it's "too late," but contrary to most of our expectations, one *can* teach old dogs new tricks, particularly if they have learned how to learn. Think about the three areas we mentioned above: education for the task, education for the system and education for society. Where do you stand in relationship to these three? What do you believe God wants you to be doing five years from now? If you haven't gone through the process of answering these questions, this is an excellent time to begin.

What About Your Personal Program?

What is it that you are going to have to learn in terms of skill or knowledge ten years from now? How will you go about learning this? Set some personal goals.

How can you integrate the gaining of new knowledge into your schedule? How many evenings or weekends a month can you set aside for formal training? Would you be better off to put yourself into an extensive one-to-three-week learning experience once a year, or to be enrolled in night classes?

Ask yourself these questions. What can you conclude from your answers?

Continuing Education Checklist

	Yes	No
I have a set of continuing education goals.	___	___
I set aside time to read at least 15 books in my field each year.	___	___
I subscribe to three or more journals or magazines in my field.	___	___
I have completed one college level course during the last twelve months.	___	___
I have thought about and done some planning for the task I will have 10 years from now.	___	___
I keep a selected reading file with me on trips away from the office.	___	___
I am an expert in one area of my field.	___	___

30

The Pattern We Gave You

Aside from the passages in Timothy and Titus, which talk about the qualifications of an elder or an overseer, it seems to us that the Bible has little to say about special qualities of Christian leaders.

But . . . the Bible does seem to indicate that the life of a Christian leader is to be such that it can be used as a model for those who follow. Consider Paul's comments to the Philippians, "But join with others in following my example, brothers, and take note of those who live according to *the pattern we gave you*" (Phil. 3:15, NIV).

There is a way of living that is first noticeable, and second, reproducible. The style and the ethos of organizations are the result of the pattern of leadership. It is certainly a pattern of management and leadership. But more importantly, it is a pattern of life.

What kind of a pattern are we giving the members of our organization? We can become so results-oriented, so production-oriented, so program-oriented that we forget we are in the business of developing people. Unlike the warrior chief who led his band into battle, most of our training is given before the battle, in the quiet times of reflection and discussion.

"Rejoice in the Lord always. I will say it again: Rejoice!" Easy to say. Difficult to do.

But we are not asked to rejoice in the environment which surrounds us. Rather, we are asked to rejoice *in the Lord*. What

Rejoice in the Lord Always

a privilege we have. First, to be in the Lord: One of Paul's favorite expressions is "in Christ." We too need to see ourselves as being in Christ, in the Lord. From a human perspective we fail continually. We make wrong decisions, bad decisions. We are discouraged by the failure of our actions to produce a desired result. We are disheartened by staff members who fail to live up to our expectations for them. We are buffeted and tossed about by problems that are not of our own making. But we are in the Lord! From this perspective, the world takes on an entirely different hue.

And we can rejoice in the Lord because He is Lord. He is Lord of all. He is the One who said I will never leave you nor forsake you. He is the One who knows the end from the beginning. He is the One who works all things together for good. It is His kingdom which reigns over all.

Hallelujah!

This is the pattern that our followers need to see in us. There may not be much in the everyday reports we are receiving in which to rejoice. But in the Lord and for the Lord there is always the potential for rejoicing. We Christians have a straightline view of history. We believe in a blessed hope. We believe that there will be a triumphant culmination of all things.

This is not to say that we should have a false enthusiasm or a hail-fellow-well-met attitude about others. Rather, it should encourage us to have a quiet confidence that though we walk through the valley of the shadow of death, He is with us. His correcting rod and His steadying staff comfort us.

Gentleness Evident to All

There are times when we have to give direct orders. There are times when we must call people to account for what they have done. There are times when we must command the attention of our followers with vigor and determination. But in all, Paul asks us to "let your gentleness be evident to all" (Phil. 4:5, NIV).

Enthusiasm, but gentleness.

Sternness, but gentleness.

Activism, but gentleness.

A demand for excellence, but gentleness.

Why gentleness? "The Lord is near" (Phil. 4:5, NIV).

The Lord is near. "He walks with us and He talks with us." His coming again is nearer today than it was yesterday. The Lord never slumbers nor sleeps. His gentleness is what He asks of us.

136

"Live according to the pattern we gave you." Have a reputation for gentleness.

Will we meet our budget this month?

Will the volunteers we need come forth?

Can I find someone who really understands how lonely it is to be in this position of leadership?

Can I keep up with this latest advance in technology?

Can we afford to send our son to college on my salary?

These are days of great anxiety. The very uncertainty of the world gives us adequate reason to be anxious. What is the antidote: "By prayer and petition, with thanksgiving, present your request to God" (Phil. 4:6b, NIV).

We are not suggesting a veneer of superficial piety. It is a truism of life that the familiar quickly becomes unrecognizable. We need a pattern. And yet we need a way of bringing to that pattern a freshness, a uniqueness that is the result of a freshness within us.

For the activists among us (probably the majority of Western Christian leaders) there is a need for us to turn our activism towards active prayer and petition. If prayer and petition are not a normal part of our everyday business, then perhaps we need to schedule them as part of that everyday business. What about leaving the last ten minutes of every meeting to ask one another what requests need to be made to God as a result of the meeting?

The world longs for leaders who have a quiet confidence that things are under control. When our private worlds are falling apart, we want desperately to know that there is somone to whom we can turn who will hold us up in the middle of our distress. When the organization is going through the storms that so often break over us, we need to turn to the person at the helm and find reassurance in calmness and control.

Rejoicing. Gentleness. No anxiety. Three pieces of the pattern. There is a fourth—contentment.

"I know what it is to be in need, and I know what it is to have plenty. I have learned the secret of being content in any and every situation, whether well-fed or hungry, whether living in plenty or in want" (Phil. 4:12, NIV).

Not a contentment with a status quo. Not a contentment that you are all right, and I don't have to be concerned for your welfare. Rather, it is a contentment that this situation right now is all right for us.

Perhaps it is easier for some of us to be content when in want. When we are in need, we tend to draw close to God and depend upon Him more. It seems much more difficult to have a feeling of dependence when budgets are being met and forecasts are being realized. Perhaps more than any other time we need to learn to be content in the midst of plenty. For it is He who gives the increase.

Finally . . .
Rejoicing. Gentleness. No anxiety. Contentment.

Nothing about effective communication or good cost control or dynamic planning. Those are all skills, along with a host of other management skills, that we can learn. Rather a quality of day-to-day living that so permeates our lives that it leaves the sweet perfume of Christ wherever we go.

"Finally, brothers, whatever is true, whatever is noble, whatever is right, whatever is pure, whatever is lovely, whatever is admirable—if anything is excellent or praiseworthy—think about such things. Whatever you have learned or received or heard from me, or *seen in me*—put in practice. And the God of peace will be with you" (Phil. 4:8, 9, NIV).

About the Authors . . .

Edward R. Dayton

As Vice-President for Mission and Evangelism, Mr. Dayton oversees ongoing policy development in this area of World Vision's work. He is responsible for the Missions Advanced Research and Communication Center (MARC), a World Vision ministry which he founded, the Research and Information division, and International projects.

After graduating from New York University with a B.S. degree in aeronautical engineering in 1948, Mr. Dayton worked in a number of engineering and management positions in the field of aircraft and space electronics systems. In his last position in this field, he was responsible for the aircraft systems, missile systems, computer systems and weapon systems departments of Lear Siegler Inc., in Grand Rapids, Michigan.

In 1964, Mr. Dayton enrolled at Fuller Theological Seminary as a full-time student. He continued as an employee of the Lear Siegler Corporation as assistant to a division president. In October 1966, he resigned his position with Lear Siegler to direct the Missions Advanced Research and Communication Center. In June 1967 he received his M.Div. degree from Fuller Theological Seminary in Pasadena, California. On July 1 of that same year MARC became a division of World Vision International of Monrovia, California.

Since joining World Vision, Mr. Dayton has traveled widely in the interest of mission strategy. He is the chairman of the Lausanne Strategy Working Group and serves on the boards of several North American and international agencies. He has written or edited over fifteen books in the area of missions and the management of Christian organizations. His most recent include *Planning Strategies for World Evangelization* and *Whatever Happened to Commitment?* He is an adjunct professor in both the School of World Mission and the Institute for Christian Organizational Development at Fuller Theological Seminary.

Mr. Dayton and his wife Marge, who is a marriage and family counselor, live in San Gabriel. They have three married daughters and a college-age son.

Ted W. Engstrom

An executive with far-ranging and finely honed skills and diverse interests, Dr. Ted W. Engstrom is a highly respected leader within the Christian community and in management circles.

As the president and chief executive officer of both World Vision International and World Vision (US) and a director on numerous boards, Engstrom is one of the most influential leaders in American religion and social service. The respect and influence come as a result of a career of notable accomplishments.

The executive vice-president since 1963 and now president of World Vision (US), Engstrom has been the guiding force in the Christian agency's phenomenal growth. Under his management-by-objective style, World Vision has significantly developed its global aid, development and evangelism programs and increased its United States support from $4 million to nearly $100 million. At the same time, overhead has remained consistently low, and the agency's fiscal responsibility and accountability are admired by many charitable organizations.

Since being named president of World Vision International, the international umbrella for World Vision's support entities in the United States, Canada, Australia, New Zealand and Europe, in October 1982, he has contributed his proven leadership skills to the overall direction of the organization. Engstrom now has the remarkable distinction of serving as president of two of the world's foremost Christian organizations. Before joining World Vision, he was for six years president of Youth for Christ International.

A sought-after management consultant, Engstrom conducted the nationwide "Managing Your Time" seminars with his colleague Ed Dayton for 10 years. He is a member of the boards of African Enterprise, the Institute of American Church Growth, Azusa Pacific University, Orval Butcher Ministries, Focus on the Family, the Luis Palau Evangelistic Association, and several other evangelical ministries. He served as the first Chairman of the Board of the Evangelical Council for Financial Accountability (ECFA) and is a member of the Presidents Association of the American Management Association.

A prolific editor and author, Engstrom has written 34 books and hundreds of magazine articles. He is the author of *The Making of a Christian Leader*, and co-author of *Managing Your Time*. A recent book is a bold call for *The Pursuit of Excellence*. His most recent book, *Your Gift of Administration*, has been published by Thomas Nelson Publishers.

Other books by Engstrom include *What in the World Is God Doing?*, *The Work Trap* (with David J. Juroe) and *Strategy for Leadership* (with Edward R. Dayton). As part of his present administrative responsibilities, he serves as publisher of *World Vision* magazine (monthly circulation over one million) and *Together*, a journal published by World Vision International.